Live Life Big or Stay in Bed

Live Life Big
or Stay in Bed

Realising and releasing your potential as a woman

HEATHER PUFFETT
& HAZEL PATTISON

MONARCH
BOOKS

OXFORD, UK & GRAND RAPIDS, MICHIGAN, USA

First published in the UK in 2010 by Monarch Books
(a publishing imprint of Lion Hudson plc)
Wilkinson House, Jordan Hill Road, Oxford OX2 8DR, England
Tel: +44 (0)1865 302750 Fax: +44 (0)1865 302757
Email: monarch@lionhudson.com www.lionhudson.com

ISBN 978 1 85424 938 8 (UK)

Distributed by:
UK: Marston Book Services, PO Box 269, Abingdon, Oxon, OX14 4YN
USA: Kregel Publications, PO Box 2607, Grand Rapids, Michigan 49501

British Library Cataloguing Data
A catalogue record for this book is available from the British Library.

Printed and bound in the UK by J.F. Print Ltd.

Dedication

I dedicate this book to my wonderful husband, Michael,
and our two beautiful daughters, Amy and Sarah.
You light up my world!
To my dad and mum, Hal and June Cable,
for always being such good
role models and for laying firm foundations in my life.
To Michael's parents, Derek and Beryl Puffett,
for being so faithful in praying for us.
Also to Granny Dor (Doreen Cable),
who has devoted much of her life to books!
Heather

I dedicate this book to my hero, Neil and our four
awesome children, Joshua, Joseph, Chloe and Tobias,
who are my greatest delight.
To my twin sister Rose and my brother Andy,
who have shared this journey with me.
To my parents, Tony and Iris Faulkner,
who have played such a significant role in laying a
foundation on which we can build.
To Pat Cook, who has mentored me
for the past twenty years.
I love you all!
Hazel

Acknowledgments

Although the content of this book is our own, it would not have been possible without the input, support, advice and encouragement of our husbands, Michael and Neil. Thank you so much for your "boots up our butts", and for spinning all those extra plates during this busy season!

A special thanks also needs to go to our beautiful children who have been incredibly patient whilst we have worked on this book – Amy and Sarah, and Joshua, Joseph, Chloe and Tobias.

Thank you to our spiritual oversight in Church of the Nations for carrying the bigger picture. Your understanding and insight into God's kingdom and the part we have to play in it, continues to inspire us.

To our spiritual dad and mum, Dave and Carol Cape, thank you for always believing in us and for cheering us on as we run the race!

Thank you to the Jubilee Eldership team for your support and encouragement. You guys are great! In fact, we would also like to thank Jubilee Church as a whole – what a brilliant family to be a part of.

Our mentoring leaders have also been truly amazing. Thank you for being so incredibly faithful in journeying with us and allowing us to speak into your lives. Without you, the mentoring programme would not be possible. Thank you also to all the ladies in Jubilee who have been a part of the mentoring. We are so grateful to those of you who have allowed us to share your stories in this book. It has been such a joy to see how you have grown through embracing His process in your lives.

Praise God for the incredible team He put around us to help with the formatting and proofreading of this book. Michael, Neil, LeeAnne, Justine, Tina, Barbara and Canja – what would we have done without you? Suzanna, your input and support has been invaluable.

The caravan in Chichester – where it all began. Thank you so much to Keith and Marjorie Pattison for allowing the use of your lovely mobile home. It has been such a place of refuge. It is where our journey began and also where we took our first steps in writing this book.

We are both so aware of our continued dependency on God. Thank You for believing in us and giving us a glimpse of Your heart to see ladies come to wholeness. We know without a shadow of a doubt that He moves – not because of us, but despite us!

Contents

Foreword

I love the statement that "every book is in some sense the product of community". This is especially true of this one. We believe that "community is a window through which people everywhere see Jesus". As I have watched Heather and Hazel develop and build community with their precious ladies, it has astounded me to see the growth, change, maturity and love that has developed.

This book is a vital resource for churches today. In a postmodern society, people are crying out for authentic, genuine relationships of trust and transparency. Many people want it; few know how to "get there". This book will help to guide you on the journey. May His kingdom come in our lives so that we would accurately reflect and represent Him in every area of society and, in this, reproduce His life in others.

Michael Puffett
Senior Pastor of Jubilee Church, Maidstone, UK
Co-author of *300+ Sizzling Icebreakers*

There is a sea of Christian books available on a range of useful subjects. Many books claim to be able to change your life, or at least declare themselves a "must-read". This book is genuinely one that needed to be written. The book builds on a foundation of mentoring works already comprehensively documented and useful as background reading. I have personally witnessed the positive change in the lives of women in Jubilee Church as a result of the application of the principles outlined here. As I read this book, I realize how many treasured principles concerning the kingdom of God were hidden to me at the start of my full-time Christian ministry, but of which I now enjoy the benefit. As you read this book, I encourage you to read beyond a mindset of models and programmes that may increase the size of your church, and apply the kingdom principles that are costly and long-lasting. Well done to my wife, Hazel, her true friend Heather, and to all the ladies who contributed to the final product.

No more the grey lives of subjugated spirits.
Let women arise and receive their place,
As they enjoy full life as co-workers in God's kingdom.

Neil Pattison
District Pastor at Jubilee Church, Maidstone, UK

Introduction

Heather writes...

Life is a journey – and definitely not a straightforward one, either! James writes in verses 2 and 3 of his first chapter, "Consider it pure joy, my brothers, *whenever* you face trials of many kinds, because you know that the testing of your faith develops perseverance" (NIV, my italics). I am sure that you have had your fair share of trials in life... Hazel and I both certainly have. These *life experiences* have a way of moulding us; shaping our thinking and our behaviour. Some experiences have a positive outworking in our lives, whilst it is true to say that other experiences leave us feeling a little worse for wear. This is the wonderful reality of life.

At the time when Hazel and I first met, we quickly discovered how much we had in common. We are both the same age (both born on the 30th), with similar aged children; we're the same height, have the same initials; we both view shopping as therapy for stress; we enjoy having a good laugh together and we even both feel comfortable when we are being less-than-our-usual sensible selves and are having one of our "blonde moments". (Not too often, though, as our husbands' exasperated sighs keep us in check!) We also both have husbands who are called to impact nations. No pressure!

When we scratched just beneath the surface, however, we realized that we also both felt battered and slightly bruised from the high expectations put on us by ourselves and by others. The desperate cry of our hearts was, "There *must* be more than this!" We began to journey side by side, and drew great comfort, strength and support from knowing that we were in it together.

This book is about our lives; our friendship, and our responsibility to offer the freedom we have found to others. Looking back, I can see how God supernaturally orchestrated the right people at the right time to cross our paths. God the Father responded to our eager hearts to be used by Him and He gave us the tools to build deep, meaningful and purposeful friendships. Hazel and I both carried the vision in our hearts to pioneer and lead a mentoring programme for women, initially within Jubilee Church and, later on, further afield. Women who, when all is stripped away, are just like us; just like you. Journey with us as we share our hearts and our lives, the ups and the downs and the lessons we have learned along the way.

Be encouraged... there *is* more than this. We have found incredible fulfilment as we have laughed and cried with many women as we have journeyed alongside them.

Some of the areas where Hazel and I have grown and then gone on to see transformation in the lives of others include:

• Knowing what it means to be part of God's kingdom; understanding our place and how we fit into the bigger picture.

• Realizing that our value and worth is found in *who we are* rather than in *what we do*. We are no longer performance-driven, because we understand that we are daughters of the King!

• Living with a deeper sense of security – we are free to be who God has created us to be and no longer live under the curse of constantly comparing ourselves to others.

• We have grasped the fact that there is great safety and security in establishing godly boundaries in our lives.

• We understand that ultimately *we* are responsible for our own growth. God provides the tools and the resources but we need to take hold of them and apply them to our own lives.

Hazel writes...

The title of this book is *Live Life Big or Stay in Bed*. Bed is great. I love my bed. It is cozy, and warm, and quiet, and safe. One of my sons probably loves his bed even more than I love mine. Getting him out of bed is a nightmare... especially on a cold school morning when he has to catch the bus in the rain. We call him "dormouse" and the name fits him well. Even on the rare occasion when we succeed in getting him out of bed he will appear with the duvet still attached to him, wound around him like a giant cocoon, and it takes more than one strong adult to prize it from his grasp.

Sometimes I get a very strong urge to stay in bed all day. I want to close myself away and sleep so that I do not have to think about anyone or anything else. Very occasionally, I have done it. But at the end of the day, when night is drawing in and the day is almost over, I feel full of regret that I have, in fact, wasted a whole day. I wonder what I have missed and what my day could have looked like if I had just got up and let it begin... if I had lived life. This book is our story of getting out of bed and living life to the full. It is our journey, one that quite simply began by getting up from our places of slumber and embarking on a road full of adventure and excitement.

Our heart in writing this book is that you will find within its pages keys, resources and inspiration to live in the fullness of all that He has intended for you. Wherever you may be on your journey, be encouraged that you are not alone and that there are others who, like you, desire to move further and deeper in their pursuit of the Father. We trust that through reading these pages, you will not only have heard the cry of a woman's heart but that you will also feel more equipped to respond to that cry. If He can use us, He can use anyone.

On a more personal note, if you had mentioned a few years ago that we would both be writing a book, we would probably have fainted! We have to say that although it has been a busy season in our lives, it has also been one of the best. We have had more fun than you could imagine. Our friendship has developed to a place where we are both completely real and transparent with one another. We have cried and laughed and, at times, even proved that we are capable of being insanely silly in an attempt to keep our heads above water!

1

A Wake-up Call

There Must Be More Than This!

by Heather and Hazel

*The great thing in this world is not so much where
we are but in what direction we are moving.*

Oliver Wendell Holmes

Hazel writes...

Friendships come in all shapes and sizes. Some
are the kind that last for ever, others just emerge
for a key season in one's life and then seem to
fizzle out. Some are intense, forged through tough times in
extreme conditions, while others seem to have been there
for ever, solid, consistent. Each one is unique, fulfilling a
different role in a different part of our lives. Friendship is
a gift from God.

The journey began for us some years ago, while we
were away on holiday together with our families. To be
honest, we hardly knew each other and were probably a
little apprehensive! We found ourselves staying together in

a caravan and a small tent, ten of us in total, in a beautiful place called West Wittering, near Chichester. In hindsight, we were both oblivious to the fact that our heavenly Father was busy planning and orchestrating on our behalf.

Have you ever been in a situation where there is an element of the divine at work? Where the Holy Spirit steps in and accelerates a process that could otherwise take years? There was a sharing of hearts and a frank openness and honesty that developed between us; it was as if God had taken two struggling individuals and caused their paths to collide.

One day, Michael, Neil and the children all decided to go out crabbing and, although we were invited, we opted to stay behind, make a pot of tea and settle down for an afternoon of getting to know one another. Although one of us came from England and the other from South Africa and our upbringings and experiences were quite different, there was a similar thread that had been woven through our lives. Sometimes it is very difficult to see the things in your own life that are holding you back. I once remember seeing a bumper sticker that read, "Blind spots kill",which I have since realized can be true for our lives too. As we chatted, we began to see the blind spots, the areas where we had been living under a lie, far from the truth of God's Word.

As Heather and I have stepped out and embraced our destinies, we have seen our own potential released. Together we are committed to see others discover their potential and see it released to achieve their God-given destinies.

Heather writes...

New Year's Day is always a great time to reflect upon the year just gone by and to set goals and resolutions for the year ahead. We all start so well but then somehow, usually even before the end of January, we find ourselves failing to live by the high standards we set ourselves. How does this make us feel? For me, words like "failure" and "defeated" come to mind. The Bible could not be clearer in stating that we are more than conquerors through Christ (Romans 8:37), yet how often do we end up feeling completely defeated in our daily lives? Then there are the lies... the many lies that the enemy constantly whispers as he seeks to gain control of our minds; lies that instil feelings of unworthiness, inadequacy, fear and insecurity.

Hazel and I both recognize now that we were living our lives under these lies. They defined who we were and who we were becoming. In reality, they left us both feeling completely bound up and ineffective in our callings. If I could describe pictorially how I was feeling at my lowest point, it would be like seeing a clip from a movie where some poor hostage is bound and gagged on a chair in the middle of a bare room. The frustration was almost unbearable and it was only as Hazel and I shared the painful truth of where we were at in our lives, that we realized we were bound by the same lies.

From the time I first met Michael, I realized that here was a man whom God could use big time. The age-old saying of "opposites attract" left me licking my wounds of inadequacy as I began the fateful journey of comparing myself with my husband. Here was a man who was not only a gifted teacher and motivational speaker, he was a visionary with the ability to pioneer new things and lead leaders. "What could I possibly bring to the table?" was the constant cry of my heart. Michael's God-given ability to motivate and release people into God's destiny seemed to have the opposite effect on me! All I wanted to do was run away and hide from the glaring expectations that I felt people had of me as "the pastor's wife". I felt that I was a disappointment both to Michael and to God. This propelled me into a season where I began to despise the ministry, as I felt as though it was driving a wedge between Michael and me. He had always been passionate about what God had called him to do and he did not seem to be waiting around for me to play catch-up! I was desperate to be a part of things but as my feelings of inadequacy grew, I began to wonder whether God could ever use me – whether He even needed me. After all, He had Michael!

In a warped way, I felt strangely comforted by the fact that Hazel was also bound by a spirit of fear and it was only through raw honesty with one another that we realized just how messed up we both were. There had been so much in Hazel's life that had terrified her; at one point, even leaving the house was a battle. Her fear of man and fear of failure overwhelmed her to the point where she began to despise herself. For me, it was only after I reached my lowest point that I was desperate enough to allow God into those secret places and bring about significant changes in my life. I believe that He sometimes allows us to journey to a place where we eventually despise where we are. I think that had I not reached rock-bottom, I would probably have lived a mediocre life way below God's original intent. For me, the road to freedom started with a firm decision and a real determination in my heart.

Hazel writes...

Although the journey is one that we have walked together, Heather and I both had different areas where God was specifically working. For me, stepping up and taking responsibility, particularly in the area of leadership, was a huge mountain to climb. Responsibility was something that had always terrified me and something I would avoid at all costs. I can remember when my children were little, taking them into town with my husband, Neil. I worried that they would get hurt by the busy road but, rather than take responsibility, I found myself shrinking back and distancing myself so far from them that I couldn't even see them, let alone ensure that they were safe! Subconsciously my thinking was probably that if any harm had come to them, it would have been Neil's fault because he was closer to them than I was. The root of this kind of behaviour was the genuine belief that I did not have what it takes, that I could not be trusted. I deeply doubted myself and my abilities.

The outcome was that I failed to step out and could not make myself fully available to God because of the fears and inadequacies that restricted me. By contrast, Heather's biggest fear was probably public speaking – actually, she avoided anything that involved being in the public eye.

We both decided to tackle our fears head-on. Heather decided to organize a ladies' conference, with the theme "Closer, Deeper, Higher", giving women an opportunity to press in and experience a greater level of intimacy in their Christian walk. It was huge bravado at the time but nine months later, as the event drew closer, she became increasingly fearful. She couldn't believe what she had done! If it was not for the fact that she had organized a speaker and some of the ladies had already registered, I think she would have called it off.

But God was faithful, despite how she was feeling. We ended up having a brilliant time away with seventy-four ladies and I know that God did a major work in her life that weekend. He imparted faith for bigger things and planted seeds of vision for launching a ladies' ministry within Jubilee Church, Maidstone.

At the conference, one of the things that came to light was that so many other women were also wrestling with similar issues. A South African lady, Edna Els, was the guest speaker at the conference. Edna was running a mentoring programme in Jeffrey's Bay, South Africa. Edna and Heather took some time out from the conference on the Saturday afternoon and Edna shared what they were doing with the ladies in her church.

Heather felt God beginning to stir something in her spirit. She knew that the timing was right for a similar work to begin in Maidstone, so decided to invite Edna back to England the following year, 2004. We also invited leaders from the various churches with which we worked in Maidstone and by the end of the training day we were all bursting with vision and excitement. It was the start of a whole new adventure and, for the first time, Heather was able to recognize the lie of the enemy that she had believed for so long... the truth was, she did have something to contribute after all!

When God begins a work in our hearts, it is never just about us. Heather and I realized that although God was busy exposing issues in our lives, we were not alone in how we were feeling. The issues we were facing were bigger than just us. We understood that the ache we carried was not just ours but that of numerous women who were trapped in loneliness and despair – women who were so hungry for the things of God and yet so bound by the yoke of inadequacy that the enemy had placed upon their shoulders; women who longed to be effective in the hands of their saviour and yet found themselves unable to rise up from the ashes and fight for their deliverance.

I have always had a love for people. I think God has used much of my life experience to shape me and plant within me a desire to see others walking in a freedom that only Christ can give them. Our freedom is a gift, bought with a terrible price and yet it is only in very recent years that I have learnt how to claim and appropriate that freedom. So much of my life was spent in the shadows, bound by the lies that the enemy had planted in my mind. I never dreamt that God could use me to speak His truth to broken lives, or that I would experience the joy of seeing others set free to fulfil their original design – I was too busy nursing my wounds and feeding my own sense of inadequacy.

Heather writes...

The lies that we believe are exposed as we discover our true identity in Christ. So, who are we? Why does the gap between who we are meant to be and who we really are seem so wide?

When my year group from high school celebrated our twenty-year reunion, I considered what it would be like, seeing old friends again. I remembered old classmates exactly as I had last seen them... and concluded that this was the way that they would also remember me.

I thought about what my personality had been like while I had been at school. One evening, over a meal at a church planting conference, I had the chance to chat to a Christian psychologist. He explained to me that over the years, one's personality does not actually change; that our personalities are mostly formed by the age of seven. In very simple terms, depending on the different circumstances that we face, we either end up erecting walls to protect ourselves, or we become experts at wearing masks to conceal our true selves for fear of being rejected. These masks come in many different forms and show themselves in many different ways. For some people loud bravado behaviour can be a mask, while for others it might be a sarcastic or relentless "sense of humour". A mask that Hazel and I have seen many times is the "invisible" mask, which allows the wearer to feel and be inconspicuous even in a crowded room. And then there is the "I am in control" mask; in control of circumstances, emotions and life in general.

I know that at conception God has a unique plan and purpose for each one of our lives. I believe that in the design of who we are, God equips us with a basic personality type in order to fulfil the destiny that He has ordained for us. If the enemy can successfully cause us to lose our identity, it will be much harder for us to fulfil the purpose for which we were created. As I reflected upon my own life, I realized that "who I was" during the first ten years of my life was very similar to who I believe I am today – and that what happened in the interim was a direct result of the enemy stealing my identity and preventing me from fulfilling God's purpose for my life.

The enemy comes only to steal, kill and destroy (John 10:10) and he had pretty much succeeded in both Hazel's and my life in almost every way. He is set on our destruction and he often does this by isolating us. The truth is that we are daughters of the risen King. Paul boldly declares in Romans 8 that if God is for us, who can be against us? Even though we are a royal priesthood, we so often live our lives with our souls in the gutter. However, in His great mercy, God rescued us from this place and He is teaching us what it means to be His daughters; to truly know Him – the One to whom we belong. It is only as we allow Him to renew our minds that we can begin to walk with our heads held high, as more than conquerors.

As we continue to be transformed, He begins to release us into the longings and dreams that have been dormant for so long. We can take our place in the dance of life and embrace His destiny for our lives. Our place in that dance is different to yours but together we can reflect the beauty of our saviour to a broken world.

Hazel writes...

Once we had discovered our true identity as daughters of the King and become secure in the fact that we belonged and were totally loved and accepted, a strange and mysterious thing occurred. A righteous anger and shaking began to rise in us, stirred from hidden places like a huge cat woken from a state of deep slumber. When revelation has done its work and the Spirit has opened your eyes to the wonders of the cross, you no longer want to return to those old places in which you have dwelt for so long. The book of Proverbs puts it another way:

> Like a dog that returns to its vomit
> Is a fool who repeats his folly.

> (Proverbs 26:11, NASB)

For Heather and I, there rose in us not only an anger for the years that the enemy had snatched from us but also a new resolve and determination to keep moving forward and not return to those old places of captivity. We were tentative and afraid of what lay ahead but we were no longer prepared to stay in the place we had been for far too long. I can clearly remember one Sunday morning sitting in church and thinking, "God, I'm terrified of changing but I'm even more terrified of staying the same." Have you ever felt like that? This was a defining moment for me. I was no longer

25

content to remain discontent. For so many years, I had been aware of the discontent I carried under the surface but felt unable to rise up from beneath it.

Have you read the Chronicles of Narnia by C. S. Lewis? One of my favourite books is *The Silver Chair*.[1]

There is a part in the story that gives a powerful illustration of deception and how the enemy holds one captive. Prince Rilian of Narnia has been taken captive for over ten years by the evil Queen of Underland and held so under her spell that all day he has no memory that he ever was a prince. But at night, for a brief period of time, he is bound to a silver chair while his mind returns to him and he cries out for his old life. The children, Jill Pole and Eustace Scrubb, along with a Marsh-wiggle called Puddleglum, have been sent by Aslan himself to rescue the prince from the queen's grasp. After many adventures, the children finally find Rilian and, having hidden and witnessed the frightening enchantment, set him free and destroy the silver chair. Rilian is shocked to hear that he has been in the power of the witch for ten years. He says that now he can remember his enchanted life but while he was enchanted, he could not remember his true self.

Once the power of darkness is broken, we see clearly and realize how the enemy has blinded us with his lies and deception.

The story continues. The Queen of Underland enters the room to discover three strangers (Jill, Eustace and a Marsh-wiggle), the silver chair destroyed and the Prince free, with his sword in his hand. Apparently unfazed by what she sees, she walks over to the fire and throws on it some green powder which produces a sweet and drowsy smell that gradually fills the room. She takes a musical instrument, rather like a mandolin, and begins to play a slow monotonous tune. The less they notice the tune, the more it gets into their heads, making it hard to think. Slowly Rilian and the children come under her spell and Lewis writes that the more enchanted one gets, the more certain one is that they are not enchanted at all.

The queen goes on to say that there never was such a place as Narnia, it was all a dream, and the children repeat this – and other things – after her. Meanwhile, Puddleglum, our Marsh-wiggle friend, is doing all he can to resist her power. He stamps his webbed, cold-blooded foot in the fire.

Three things happen all at once. The sweet sickly smell becomes greatly less, the queen cries out in horror and Puddleglum, because of the pain in his foot, suddenly gets a clear head and sees things as they really are! All this breaks the spell and Prince Rilian and the children are free again. As a result, they are able to fight off the evil and overcome.

I think this is such a brilliant illustration of how the enemy seeks to allure us into a place of captivity and then hold us captive with his lies. The longer we believe them, the more hold they have over us, becoming established as truth in our lives. Sometimes we need to hear someone shout "Wake up!" and rouse us from a state of slumber.

Awake, you who sleep,
Arise from the dead,
And Christ will give you light.

(Ephesians 5:14, NKJV)

It's talking here of a state of spiritual slumber that makes us vulnerable to the snares of the enemy. If we are not careful, we can be lured into a false sense of security and find ourselves out of the race, passive and indifferent to the purposes of God. Praise God, it was as if He had clapped His hands over Heather and I and shouted "Wake up!" to our souls. Things were beginning to stir. We were beginning to get out of our beds, our places of apathy, and a growing desire to start really "living life" began to push its way to the surface.

Heather had tried everything, from resisting her calling, to trying to remain invisible. The only thing left for her to do was to press into God as if her very life depended on it. This was for her a key turning point; a decision of the heart that enabled God to break in and bring transformation from the inside out. She began to find God in a new way, with a fresh understanding that it was not what she could do *for* Him but rather *who she was in Him*. This understanding brought great healing. She attended a conference during this time and had an opportunity to receive prayer ministry from some key leaders. Heather received a prophetic word saying, "God wants to do heart surgery; He wants to cut out those areas where you have hardened your heart and give you a new heart." I have personally witnessed this work of restoration taking place in Heather's heart and she is a testimony to the goodness and faithfulness of her God.

Each one of us is responsible for our own walk with the Lord – no one can walk it for us. No one is going to miraculously change our circumstances, or take away the hurdles that we face, but rather we need the courage to face them head-on, one by one. I can remember a time when I was too afraid to drive as a result of a car accident that I had been in twenty years previously. It had held me back for years and had been an area where I felt very ashamed and defeated. This was one of those things that I had to face, overcoming gut-wrenching fear and putting myself literally in the driving seat. Initially it was immensely hard and the physical manifestation of fear left me shaking, with my knuckles white on the steering wheel. However, I would get in, speak loudly to my soul that "I can do all things through Christ who strengthens me" (Philippians 4:13, NKJV) and start up the engine. On the bad days when I felt like the fear really had a grip, I would force myself to drive even if I had nowhere to go. I would turn up at unsuspecting friends' houses demanding a big cup of strong coffee. No one could do it for me but as He enabled me, I was able to face the monster and deal with it. As we allow Him in, He gives us the strength to overcome. When we fully surrender to Jesus there is no telling where it will take us but one thing is for sure – it is a road to freedom.

As I sit here, my heart is racing with excitement and anticipation. Heather and I share such a deep desire to see you, God's women, released into the plans and purposes that He has for you. Although we may not know you by name, we see that untapped potential, those unfulfilled dreams and desires that lie in the secret places of your hearts. We understand those longings for deeper friendships, accountability and a safe place where you can afford to be vulnerable. We are familiar with a cry that rises up from the depths of your being that says, "There must be more than this." You are not alone; countless others echo your cry.

God's Spirit is moving to and fro across the earth, searching for hearts who will respond. Are you willing? Will you stand up and allow Him to use you, despite the whispers of inadequacy you may be hearing? You will need His strength to guide you and His grace to enable you. You will need to learn to fight like you have never fought before but you will also learn to overcome. The challenges never stop and each day we choose to move forward rather than shrink back into those dark places. But we have a great cloud of witnesses who are cheering us on, willing us to keep going, shouting from the wings, "Never give up, keep going, run the race and win the prize!"

The prize ultimately is Jesus, our saviour and our King, the One who makes it all worthwhile. But on a day-to-day basis, the prize probably looks different to each one of us. For Heather and I, the prize is found in knowing our true identity in Christ, in the realization that we have potential, in the joy of seeing that potential released and in the privilege of seeing it unlocked in the lives of others.

NOTE

1 C. S. Lewis, *The Silver Chair* London: Fontana Lions, 1980. First published 1953 by Geoffrey Bles.

2

Kissing the Comfort Zone Goodbye

Discovering Our Potential

by Heather and Hazel

Your potential is much greater than what you are right now.

Dr Myles Munroe

Hazel writes...

I have a mobile phone. So does my husband and so do three of my four children. The youngest is desperate to have one but we are trying to hold off for as long as possible! I use my phone for calling people and for sending text messages. I love my phone. I use it every day, I understand how it works and I am confident with it. I have always had a Nokia phone and I always will... I *get* Nokia. However, the other members of my family all have different types of phones. They use theirs not just for making calls and sending texts but for playing games, listening to music and even as a torch to light their way home! I don't *get* their phones. I don't get what they do on them and, to be honest, I am a little scared of them. Sometimes, if I am running low on credit, Neil will give me his phone to use and within five minutes I want to throw it at the wall!

When I use my phone, I am in my comfort zone. It does not challenge me or test my patience. It is safe and reliable, predictable and familiar. There is a whole part of my phone that I never use... I don't even know what it's capable of. It takes time and effort to learn the workings of a phone, especially if you are anything like me, but when you discover that little something new you never want to go back to the old way of doing it. Take predictive texting for example. Initially it is terrifying but as you persevere, you quickly learn that it is a far quicker way to send a message. The only way for me to advance in my phone skills is to kiss my comfort zone goodbye and take the plunge. I am surrounded by a family who are seriously clued into mobile phone technology and they are patient (even if at times exasperated) teachers. It is a humbling experience to be taught by a twelve-year-old! It is a silly illustration but don't you think this is often how we live our lives, way below our potential and ignorant of what we are really capable of?

Our flesh enjoys being comfortable and yet comfort can be one of the most crippling things for us if we want to reach out and achieve our God-given potential. Being "comfortable" can lure us into a false sense of security and can cause us to function way below the level for which we were created. When I look at the life Jesus lived here on the earth, there is not much I see that appeared comfortable. He did not even have a pillow on which to lay His head. He did not enjoy many luxuries but rather lived simply, that others might simply live. Comfort zones not only apply to the physical state of things, but also to a state of mind that can make us passive and lethargic. As God shook us, Heather and I had a choice to either remain in that place of comfort, or to step outside of all we considered familiar and safe. In order for our untapped potential to be discovered and fulfilled, we needed to be willing to move out from the comfortable into unknown territory. We had to move away from the old in order to embrace the new.

As I was growing up, I was aware that there was a certain kind of mould for women. There was a dress code, a behavioural code, even a "this is how you are to relate to Jesus as a woman" code! In some churches, the women made the tea and coffee, they prepared communion and they placed the correct hymn numbers on the hymn board. They ran Sunday school (as if being with their kids all week wasn't enough!), arranged the flowers, and prepared a Sunday roast for their family. There seemed to be no alternative outlets for gifting and most contributions appeared to be made purely on a practical level.

There was almost a heaviness that seemed to clothe me, a whole part of my purpose lying dormant and hidden. I felt trapped and unfulfilled. For so many years, I was unaware of the fact that I have something unique to contribute. Our enemy will do all he can to keep us ignorant, full of self-doubt, inadequacy and worthlessness.

The truth is that each one of us possesses the inherent capacity for growth and development and yet many of us live way below our potential. There is a part of our being that is latent, waiting to come into existence, lying just beneath the surface. It requires the right keys, the right tools and the right moments to emerge. The keys are the realizations that come to us in quiet pockets of time; new understandings, revelations that provide a glimpse of a different way of living. The tools are given by others, those who can see beyond what we see and are able to call forth the potential within us. They believe in us and help to equip us by sharing their God-given resources. The moments when these things occur are determined partly by our responses, partly by others' commitment to us, but also by God's providential working in our lives. By providence, I mean the care, guardianship and control exercised by God; divine direction by a good and loving Father. These three things – the keys, the tools and God's providence – operating together, release our potential.

The potential of something is determined by its source. But the problem is that often we do not know, or fully understand, our true source and therefore are never able to fully enter in. When we begin to grasp the implications of God's words in Genesis 1:26, "Let us make man in our image" (NIV) and see that *He* is our source, then we take a significant step forward on our journey to freedom.

Heather and I saw very quickly that it was much easier to spot potential in each other than in ourselves. We found it easier to say "I believe in you" than "I believe in myself".

Not only did we need to admit that we had comfort zones but we also had to recognize the fact that we had set things in place to guard and protect them. I had a fear of stepping out and therefore had mechanisms in place in order to avoid it. Responsibility terrified me and so I abdicated it.

I can remember, having made the conscious decision to step out and embrace whatever God had for me, a season in my life where things became quite intense. I decided that for a year or two I would agree to do whatever Michael and Heather asked me to as far as my role in leadership at Jubilee Church was concerned. I gave them free rein to push and challenge me and boy, did they take me at my word! I embarked on a journey of stepping out and doing all sorts of crazy and scary things. I had to organize a large Church of the Nations conference and speak in numerous public forums, ranging from Sunday celebrations to meetings with members of the local council. I went from an "I can't do it" mentality to one of "I can do *all* things through Christ who strengthens me" (Philippians 4:13, NKJV, my italics). There were plenty of tears and sweat and panic but God was so faithful and I experienced intense personal growth. I was fast-tracked to a place of wholeness that I had not thought possible before. Seeing how Heather and Michael believed in me, even in the times where I could not see it for myself, spurred me on and gave me the chance to soar. Potential needs a pressure pot to grow and be released from, which is why it is often not realized. It is usually a combination of other people in our lives and our circumstances that causes this to happen. It is an uncomfortable process but one that we need to embrace. It will be well worth it.

Heather writes...

I agree wholeheartedly with Hazel in that our flesh constantly cries out for comfort. Two things that I used to avoid in order to remain comfortable were public speaking (although I believe that this is one of humanity's most common fears) and confrontation. Both of these fears blocked the way forward for me to reach my full potential and I only experienced growth in these areas when I was prepared to lay down my need for comfort. I needed to determine how desperate I was for breakthrough in these areas. As I pondered my options, I realized that in choosing the more difficult road, the liberty that comes with breakthrough would far outweigh the risks I had perceived. I also became aware that the support and encouragement from my family and friends were essential tools in removing the obstacles that blocked my path. They believed in me and they could see my potential when I wasn't able to.

What does it mean to believe in someone? I mean, to *truly* believe in someone? As a mother, I know that I love both my daughters unconditionally. In other words, despite what they may or may not do, I will *always* love them. In fact, it is such a deep love that I know that if it came to it, I would give my life for them. However, this does not necessarily mean that we ooze gushing love for one another 24/7. In the real world, there are times when I feel as though I need a little space – not often, though; only when the tension builds to near breaking point! Michael always teases about the hard lot he has been dealt in life, having to live with three women in the same house! And yet, even though he jests, he would give his life for us. The reality is, the closer a relationship, the more it is tested. It is often those we are closest to – our families – that bear the brunt of who we really are; with them, we wear no masks at all. And yet we still love so deeply... so unconditionally. Loving our children means that we will *always* believe in them, *always* want the best for them and that we will do everything within us to enable them to reach their full potential.

Believing in our children enables us to look past their shortcomings and failings to see their potential.

Although friendship is different to a mother/daughter relationship, I believe it is based on similar principles. Friendships too undergo testing as it is only in the tough times that we can determine just how deep the relationship really is. Our loyalty to one another is not tested when things are going well; it is only when we have had a chance to walk away and choose not to that we can be considered

36

a loyal friend. Sadly, some friendships do not withstand the pressure that testing brings and through life's ups and downs we seem to flow in and out of relationships. The friendships that do survive serious testing are rare and precious and when tough times come, these are the friends who will still be on the sideline cheering us on. These are the friends who continue to believe in us despite our failings and shortcomings. These are the friendships that we need to guard and press in to; the friendships that we *really need* when real life happens!

One of the tactics of the enemy is to bring us into isolation as we are much more vulnerable when we are on our own. We can see this principle in operation amongst wild animals. Have you ever seen a lioness stalking her prey? She will always go for the youngest or weakest animal, or she will target those that have been separated from the rest of the herd. The enemy is delighted when we walk away from a friendship because we have been offended.

The incredible friendship that Hazel and I benefit from is a result of the seasons of testing that we have experienced. There was a time where circumstances caused me to question Hazel's loyalty towards me. I cannot deny that during this time I felt incredibly vulnerable and afraid that this was a testing that our friendship would not survive. There was a short period where all I wanted to do was withdraw and isolate myself; perhaps this was even necessary for a short season. I also knew that the longer an issue remains unresolved, the worse it becomes. Time, like a magnifying glass, has the potential to cause an issue to grow and fester. I withdrew just long enough to get a grip on my emotions as I did not want them to cloud my judgment of the situation. The truth was, I knew Hazel well enough to know her heart and that the circumstances that resulted in my doubts were completely beyond her control. I could so easily have remained *boxed in* by my offence.

The Greek word for "offence" is *skandalon* which literally means the trigger of a trap, or a trap stick. As a young boy, Michael used to love catching birds in his garden. He would tie a piece of string to a stick and then rest a shoebox on its side, balancing on the stick. As soon as a poor, unsuspecting bird hopped for the bait under the box, he would tug on the piece of string and pull the stick out from under the box. The desired result would be a bird caught under the box. When we are offended, the *skandalon* (trap stick) has been tripped and the box has dropped. Have you ever had the "box of offence" over your head? When the girls were younger, they loved playing in and making houses out of boxes. I have had a cardboard box over my head and from first-hand experience, I can testify to the fact that not only is it dark under the box but there is also a definite sense of being disorientated. Offence has the same result. In the "dark" we are not able to think clearly or rationally and our judgment becomes clouded by our emotions. It is only when we come out from under the box, back into the light, that we are able to gain a clearer perspective on the situation.

Offence is always rooted in initial hurt. I had felt hurt by the circumstances that Hazel and I found ourselves in. It was only after I *came out from under the box* that I was able to see more clearly and, more importantly, hear God's heart on the situation. Hazel and I had already walked a long road together and neither of us were prepared to walk away. I know that during this time, Hazel also felt incredibly vulnerable; desperate for me to understand her actions. I knew I had to confront the situation and talk openly and honestly about how I was feeling. Hurts that are pushed down always manage to find a way of resurfacing in the future – usually with a dose of bitterness added to the equation. I soon realized that her hands had been completely tied and that God's timing, as usual, had been perfect. Both our hearts were broken as we realized the potential that the enemy had to destroy our relationship. As I chose to walk in forgiveness, He gave me courage to trust once again. We came so close to losing what we believe to be a gift of friendship from God. As we weathered that particular storm we both grew stronger and our level of respect for one another definitely deepened.

I thank God that despite all that happened, we both continue to believe in one another. By God's grace, we are able to see beyond our shortcomings and focus on the potential we see in each other. We are all "works in progress", working out our salvation on a daily basis. I am greatly comforted by the fact that we are not called to journey through life alone and am so thankful that God has blessed me with an incredible family and friends who love and support me. On the days when it feels as though the darkness is closing in, it is our closest friends who walk alongside us, who steer us towards the light once again. The writer of Proverbs 18:24 says, "A man of many companions may come to ruin, but there is a friend who sticks closer than a brother" (NIV). I am so grateful to God that within His design, He has within us a need for one another. We are not "lone rangers".

Kissing my comfort zone goodbye has not been easy, but has definitely been worth the feeling of being out on a limb. Looking back on the early days, I realize now that I was probably a real pushover; easily hurt, with many emotions that remained bottled up. I now enjoy an amazing sense of freedom as I have learned to rise up in the full potential of who God created me to be.

3

If You Want a Friend...
Be a Friend!

Foundations for Godly Friendships

by Hazel

Community is the window through which the world
sees Jesus.

Michael Puffett

All genuine friendships go through a time of testing
and, as Heather has mentioned, ours has been no
exception. The incident that Heather has briefly
recounted was very painful for both of us and yet today
we are able to share a friendship that is safe and secure.
We choose to believe the best in one another, to keep short
accounts and to be as transparent as possible. If the enemy
can destroy trust between friends, he has succeeded in
destroying the very root. Without trust, nothing of any
substance can be built.

There is such a hunger in our hearts for meaningful
friendships. Why is this?

God our Father is relational and consequently we, as His

precious children, also carry this attribute. He has placed within each one of our hearts the need for relationship, both with Himself as our Father and with one another.

Genesis 2:18 says, "The Lord God said, 'It is not good for the man to be alone. ...'" (NIV). God created us with the fundamental need for intimacy. This was His original plan and design for humankind and it remains the same today. This essential part of our make-up, our DNA, is one of the things that set us apart from the rest of creation.

When Jesus walked the earth, He explained to those close to Him that He desired friendship and not a relationship based on fear or a sense of duty. Jesus said, "I no longer call you servants, because a servant does not know his master's business. Instead, I have called you friends, for everything that I learned from my Father I have made known to you" (John 15:15, NIV).

Jesus, the Son of God, desires an intimate relationship with us. He longs to reveal to us the Father's heart and share with us on a deeply personal level, one of a close friend. He wants us to know Him, to listen to the beat of His heart and to hear Him whisper His words of love to us. He calls us by name, invites us to come, to be quieted in His love, and to listen as He rejoices over us with singing (Zephaniah 3:17, NKJV).

There is probably no greater expression of love for a friend than the laying down of one's life. But Christ goes a step further, laying down His life for us while we were still His enemies:

> But God demonstrates His own love for us in this:
> While we were still sinners, Christ died for us. Since
> we have now been justified by his blood, how much
> more shall we be saved from God's wrath through

him! For if, when we were God's enemies, we were reconciled to him through the death of his Son, how much more, having been reconciled, shall we be saved through his life!

(Romans 5:8–10, NIV)

It is amazing to think that it was during the time when we were furthest away from His loving arms that Christ went to the cross for us. How often do we fall into thinking "when I'm good enough I will return to Him"? The truth is that it is in this very position as "sinner" that He first reaches out to us and beckons us home.

Matthew Henry says the following in his commentary:

Jesus loved His disciples and took them into a covenant of friendship with Himself. They had proved to Him their sense of duty and servanthood, and therefore they were admitted and advanced to the dignity of His friends. Christ takes believers to be His friends. He visits them and converses with them as His friends, bears with them and makes the best of them, is afflicted in their afflictions and takes pleasure in their prosperity; He pleads for them in heaven and takes care of all their interests there. He is a friend that loves at all times. He calls us friends, and not only loves us but lets us know it![1]

If we can grasp the reality – that He wants to be our friend – we will be for ever changed. This friendship, the most vital and significant relationship in our lives, will not disappoint or fade. With such a revelation comes a transformation of the heart that enables us to *be* a friend to others. Friendship with Jesus is the best kind. He loves at all times; He has our

42

very best interests at heart; He hurts when we are hurting; He is the first to rejoice in our successes.

Consequently, our friendships can flow from a place of wholeness, peace and quiet confidence, radiating His love and beauty. In a world where so many people struggle with feelings of loneliness, we are able to bring the incredible gift of healthy, godly friendships. The message of hope, life in abundance, and the joy of His Spirit in us are just a few of the truths that we can carry to hurting hearts.

He has designed us to need not only intimacy with Him but also to need one another. How often have you heard someone say that it is "just God and me, thank you very much"? This is a protection mechanism that we often display in an attempt to keep our hearts from being wounded – we put up the walls and hope that in isolating ourselves we will be free from hurt. We can live in the deception that putting up these walls and hardening our hearts is sufficient to live life, but in reality we are empty and unfulfilled.

We can live in the deception that putting up these walls and hardening our hearts is sufficient to live life but in reality, we are empty and unfulfilled. This is a far cry from God's best for our lives; we miss out on so much if we become content to just exist in loneliness or in superficial friendships, for fear of being hurt or let down. I went through a season in my life where I remember making a conscious decision to let no one in to my private world. Having been let down and disappointed, I thought it would be easier to just put up walls. I would watch from the sidelines as my peers got together and hung out. It was as if I was there but not *really* there. I hardened my heart and remember saying to myself, "Enough of all this crying, no more tears." This led to over a year of refusing to cry or release my emotions; eventually, I would wake in the night sobbing for no obvious reason – but the pain had to work its way out somewhere and somehow. Instead of finding comfort in that place of isolation, I found greater heartache and loneliness.

Friendship with Christ is the best foundation and it is from this place that our other friendships can flow in wholeness and peace. He alone can free us from the fear of rejection and enable us to love again. Jesus, again and again, links love for God with love for one another and makes it quite clear that the two cannot be separated (John 15:12; 1 John 4:20). If we say that we are intimate with God, we are suggesting that we know Him and, if we know Him, we must be aware that He desires closeness with His people. He also asks us to "love one another" and to prefer one another – Romans 12:10 says "Be kindly affectionate to one another with brotherly love, in honour giving preference to one another" (NKJV). Love for someone implies trust, which leads to vulnerability, which results in intimacy.

In 1 Peter 4:8 (NKJV) we read, "And above all things have fervent love for one another, for 'love will cover a multitude of sins.'" It is essential that we face and deal with those who have hurt us and let us down. We can only walk free in our friendships if we live a lifestyle of forgiveness and learn to keep short accounts with one another. However good and kind our friends may be, the truth is that at some point, they will let us down.

Heather and I have realized that in the area of friendship, so much of its success is determined by the choices we make and the grace that we extend to one another. We blow it. We fail. We let each other down. Yet we choose to believe the best, forgive one another and cover each other's weaknesses. When we forgive those who have hurt us, we are not saying that what they have done to us does not matter; instead, we are choosing to release them and entrust them to God's righteous judgment. Holding on to and harbouring hurts and resentments are destructive and prevent us from being able to receive forgiveness and healing in our own lives. Jesus commands us to forgive one another; therefore, it must be possible, however difficult it may seem at times. Forgiveness is a choice, not a feeling or emotion. We do not need to wait until we "feel" like forgiving; otherwise it will probably never happen! It is an act of the will in direct obedience to the Word of God (Matthew 6:12, 14–15).

> You are my friends if you do what I command.
>
> (John 15:14, NIV)

People have always been my passion. While others had hobbies such as horse riding and ice skating, I was far happier just to "people watch" and observe! I longed to connect, to somehow climb into their world and see things from their perspective. I believe this passion for people is a God-given gift, not something I have had to work at or engineer – it just flows out of who He has made me to be. I recognize, however, that from an early age the enemy hijacked this gift and I went from being a "people-lover" to being a "people-pleaser".

This can be a trap for many of us and, if we are not aware of what is going on, we can begin to look to people and friendships to fulfil our need to be loved and accepted.

My whole identity and security became based on whether or not I had friends. I became so desperate that in the end I was prepared to compromise almost anything in order to be loved and accepted – even those things most precious to me. I would find myself a part of something I neither believed in nor agreed with but I joined in for fear of losing the "friendship". One day in school some friends told me they were going to the playing fields over the road to smoke cigarettes. I really did not want to go and was terrified of getting caught but my need to be accepted compelled me. I felt sick with nerves but covered it well by being funny. My sense of humour became a weapon rather than a blessing and I learned that by being sarcastic I could make people laugh. There was a sharp edge to what I said which was hilarious unless you were on the receiving end of it. We made it across the road, hearts pounding and egos growing by the minute. We sat on some huge grass rollers and soon we were lighting up and patting ourselves on the back. On the surface, we were very cool and triumphant but inside I knew that these "friends" didn't know me at all. I felt trapped. I became disappointed, felt more desperate, tried a bit harder, felt more rejected, and so the destructive cycle continued. Due to insecurities and an inability to be at peace within myself, my friendships were superficial. They became, over the years, full of conditions and "no entry" signs. My love for others became wary, suspicious and reserved. I hardened my heart and all the love and tenderness that Christ had placed within me froze over and became impenetrable.

This pattern was only broken in my life after the love of Jesus swept in and literally *ruined* me for this world. I can remember the day when I got on my knees and begged Him to free me from such a place of bondage! He whispered into my heart, "I have ruined you for this world. You will never fit in here because you don't belong here! I have made you for another place. Only in me can the ache in your heart be healed." It's like John says:

If you lived on the world's terms, the world would
love you as one of its own. But since I picked you
to live on God's terms and no longer on the world's
terms, the world is going to hate you.

(*John 15:18–19*, THE MESSAGE)

We can be so busy searching to find our place in the wrong
place and then feel confused when we are unable to press
in and feel a part of things. The revelation comes when we
understand that we were not put here to just have our needs
met by others, or to purely satisfy the selfish gratifications
of the flesh. The very thing that God has placed within us
– to be a blessing to others – is what the enemy seeks to
take and twist to become nothing short of a curse. Thank
God that "He who is in [us] is greater than he who is in the
world" (1 John 4:4, NKJV).

The world's way of building relationships can tend to
be founded on "self" and "need". You see, if God is not
Lord of our hearts, then the reality usually is that *we are*!
When we approach a relationship from a place of "What
can you give to me?" or "Do you have what I need?" the
friendship is unlikely to withstand the test of time because
the foundations are all wrong.

When our friendships are "need-based", we have a
tendency to hold on to them tightly for fear of being let
down or rejected. But sadly, we almost always lose that
which we hold on to too tightly. Such relationships, instead
of bringing life and joy, prove to be draining and often carry
a "heavy" edge. In this place of brokenness we become
dysfunctional and the desperation with which we crave
friends can become all-consuming. To feel "desperate" in
our friendships proves to be a very rocky foundation. The
definition of desperate is:

47

1. Having lost all hope; despairing.

2. Marked by, arising from, or showing despair: *the desperate look of hunger; a desperate cry for help.*

3. Reckless or violent because of despair.

4. Undertaken out of extreme urgency or as a last resort.

5. Nearly hopeless; critical.

6. Suffering or driven by great need or distress: *desperate for recognition.*

7. Extremely intense.[2]

I have seen this kind of desperation particularly in the area of boyfriend/girlfriend relationships, where girls are desperate to feel loved and accepted and almost smother the poor unsuspecting man. She clings to him like a little limpet and in the end he shakes her off because she is pinching his arm too tightly. The look of hunger in her eyes sends him running in fear. The extremely intense look on her face and the need for recognition results in him packing his bags and getting the next plane out of there! Do you remember the film *Fatal Attraction* where eventually Glenn Close becomes recklessly violent as a result of the despair she feels at the thought of losing Michael Douglas?

Where God our Father creates hearts to love and care, the enemy will do all he can to distort them into hearts that crave love and care from others. As soon as Satan can get us to focus on "me" rather than on others, he gains an access point into our hearts.

I believe that there are two good foundations that enable us to experience godly friendships and protect us from the schemes of the devil.

1. Dying to Self: The Beginning of Freedom

The path to true freedom is in surrendering that which we think is important, for that which is really important... the surrendering of "self" for the joy of Christ living in us. Wherever possible, the enemy wants to get us to focus on self. This is because *self* can never be satisfied; it is insatiable, all-consuming and results in self-destruction.

> *I* have been crucified with Christ and *I* no longer
> live, but Christ lives in me. The life I live in the body,
> I live by faith in the Son of God, who loved me and
> gave Himself for me.
>
> (*Galatians 2:20, NIV, my italics*)

This is the only place where true freedom can begin! We can become obsessed with self, but as we put self to death we can start to live in the place of inner peace that He has for us. Our flesh is demanding and the more you feed it, the hungrier it becomes (just try fasting for a few days and you will see how good it is at making its presence felt). We must put it to death daily. Being selfless is the removal of self. Obedience to the Holy Spirit leads us to operate in a way that puts others first and allows us to carry out actions that benefit others without any benefit to ourselves. Jesus, our example, lived a lifestyle like this and, as we grow more like Him, the fruit of His Spirit is produced in us too. As we are led by the Spirit we learn to lay down our lives for others. It no longer needs to benefit us in order for it to be beneficial.

2. Take Your Place as a Daughter of the King: Know to Whom You Belong

You are My beloved Son, in You I am well-pleased.

(Luke 3:22, NASB)

Here God establishes Christ's true identity: "You are *My beloved* Son..." (my italics)

Jesus had a clear sense of His identity. He knew who He was and He knew who had sent Him. He found His identity in His relationship with His Father. In these moments, just after His baptism and before He was led into the wilderness, Jesus received public recognition and was acknowledged by His heavenly Father.

We all need to know the assurance that we are His, that we belong to Him and that He delights in us. This has to be a fundamental truth that is set in our hearts. This is what we hold on to, what we cling to.

Do you know that you are your Father's daughter? Without this revelation there will always be restlessness in our souls, a questioning and lack of inner peace. In the true knowledge of being His, we can find peace and security. From this place we are able to have realistic expectations of others rather than ones that are totally unattainable.

I can remember when I first met my husband, Neil. It was during a season in which I had little knowledge of what it meant to be a "Daughter of the King". I really needed rescuing! Although God used Neil enormously in bringing healing and restoration to my life, I am very aware now that he was not the one who was able to rescue me. There were times early on in our relationship when I think I might have expected him to; however, he was very firm about the fact that he could be my hero but not my saviour.

One evening, early in our marriage, I remember going out with some friends to a quaint little pub for a drink. We were sitting round the candle-lit table chatting, when one of them asked Neil the question, "Why did you marry Hazel? What made you choose her?" In my mind I was already playing back his answer: "She's so beautiful, she was the only woman for me, she completes me, she captivated me..." The answer he gave almost knocked me off my seat. He said, "Firstly, God told me very clearly to marry Hazel and secondly, two are more effective than one in extending the kingdom of God. Together we can have a greater impact on lives and nations."

"What? What's that got to do with anything?" I thought. He could have picked any old woman off the shelf if that was all he wanted! So I was just an act of obedience, was I? I was hurt and angry, totally mortified and offended.

Looking back now, I am so grateful to Neil for not trying to take God's place in my life. I thought that in getting married I would find peace and security and that I would no longer wrestle with feelings of inadequacy. I thought that when I was married my low self-esteem would suddenly disappear. Big mistake! I was shocked to discover that after we had walked down the aisle, placed rings on fingers and uttered vows before God, I still felt so alone! I thought that once Neil had married me, I would feel better about myself and my secret self-loathing would just go away. But it did not.

You see, what I failed to understand was that I do not *belong* to Neil. I have been entrusted into his care and therefore he has a godly responsibility to me as his wife, to love and to cherish me. But I *belong* to another first and foremost – Jesus Christ, Lover of my soul. It is here that my true identity is rooted and established. I have a strong tower, a place of refuge and a shelter from the storm – His Name is Jesus!

> And my God shall supply all your need according to His riches in glory by Christ Jesus.
>
> (Philippians 4:19, NKJV)

My husband and my close friends are wonderful gifts to me but they cannot give me my sense of identity or self-worth. This needs to be found in Christ alone. I must clarify that Neil does find me beautiful (!) but this was not why he chose me as his wife. Praise God for that!

Once the foundation stones of dying to self and knowing to whom we belong are rooted in our lives, we can begin to experience a new measure of freedom in our friendships. Fear is removed from our relationships because we are secure in who we are – daughters of the King. Although our friendships may mean the world to us, they do not become our world. We begin to see a bigger picture that goes far beyond "self". We are free to be a blessing to those around us, loving unreservedly and wholeheartedly. We can afford to love extravagantly because our love no longer has to be carefully measured or withheld. Our friendships become secure and stable. We are no longer threatened by others but can share those who are precious to us with others without the fear of losing them.

When my daughter was younger she would get very stressed because she could not cope with the pressure of having to have a "best friend". Everyone had a best friend and one of the first questions a five-year-old girl will ask another is, "Who is your best friend?" She wasn't particularly worried about having a best friend, but it was almost expected. She would agonize over the question but struggled to make a decision because she would say, "I like everyone, just in a different way." I think, in the end, she decided to whisper in each child's ear, "You are my best friend" and hope that they were satisfied; after all, in her mind that was the truth – they were all best! Young children, particularly girls, place a lot of emphasis on "best" friends but as we mature we should be able to appreciate the rich variety that different friendships can bring. Every friendship brings something different because each one of us is different and contributes something unique to the relationship.

So, once we have had the revelation of being daughters of the King and understood that dying to self is the beginning of freedom, what should our friendships look like?

1. We Need to Be Available and Approachable People

Once we are confident of our true identity in Christ, our sharp edges begin to fade. As He heals the wounds of the past and forgives us for the mistakes we have made, we become secure in the knowledge that we belong, that we are loved and accepted. Insecure people are not very attractive to be around – trust me – I have been around me for forty years! But as we enter that place of belonging, there is an attractiveness that radiates from us. Others are naturally drawn to us, to *Christ in us*, and we are free to give away that which He has deposited in our hearts. We can love because "He first loved us" and we see that it truly is more "blessed to give than to receive" (Acts 20:35, NIV).

I see such a stark contrast now in the way that I view friendships and as Jesus has healed me, I have been released to be a friend to others. The title of this chapter is, "If You

Want a Friend… Be a Friend!" It is a great place to start and you will be amazed at what you reap in your own life as a result. For meaningful friendships to develop, we need to be willing to invest our time and efforts. Only over time can anything significant be built and this involves making ourselves available. We have to prioritize if we are serious about establishing these sorts of friendships.

I said to a friend recently that I felt like throwing a party; a celebration of friendship, because I did not want to take for granted that which He has given me. He has freed me from the bondage of "people-pleaser" and restored to me the gift of "people-lover"!

My life has been enriched in the last few years because I have finally been set free to pour my life into others. There are no hidden agendas or ulterior motives. As I have begun to look at my friendships from the 'how can I be a blessing to you' perspective, I have received so much back in return.

> Give, and it will be given to you: good measure,
> pressed down, shaken together, and running over
> will be put into your bosom. For with the same
> measure that you use, it will be measured back to
> you.
>
> (Luke 6:38, NKJV)

2. Be Someone Whose Hunger for the Things of God Makes Others Hungry

There is something that draws me to other women who are running their race, eyes fixed on Jesus, willingly counting the cost and passionate about their King. Part of what we bring to our friendships should be a spurring on of one another, cheering each other on in our Christian walk. There are ladies in my life who, by carrying the attributes and nature of their Father, draw me to the "Christ in them". I just love being around them because, having spent time with them, I feel as if I have encountered my saviour too.

Many years ago, there was a lady in our church called Pat Cook who was a missionary in Afghanistan. She was and still is an absolute powerhouse. She would come home to the UK from her adventures and share her incredible experiences with us on a Sunday morning. The times she had been held at gunpoint, the miraculous stories of angels protecting her and the excitement and passion she carried for Jesus were spellbinding and I would sit on the edge of my seat! I was quite young, maybe fourteen, and she was over thirty years my senior but I felt drawn to her and the God she served. She would always start and finish her times of sharing with this phrase, "You pray, I go, God does the work." When I was eighteen, I wrote and asked her if she would mentor me and we have walked a road together ever since. We have seasons where we spend lots of time together and others where we barely speak, but whenever we sit together our lives are enriched. She is so real, so wise, and her hunger for the things of God ignite a hunger in me. I am grateful that she made room for me in her busy life, especially back in those years where I was so needing direction and encouragement. She always made time for me and I would come away feeling as though I had someone who was spurring me on in my journey.

I feel so blessed now, at Jubilee Church, to be part of a leadership where I am surrounded by others who are hungry for the things of God. It is much harder to lose your spiritual appetite when all around there are others who are feasting from the same tree of delights. Sometimes I will come to a meeting feeling weary and a little dry but together we are able to pull one another to a higher level. There is such a refreshing that comes when we are fed and watered by the One who draws us and we remember that we are there because of Him and for the sake of His kingdom.

We need to let our hunger and passion for the things of God draw others to us, to *Him* in us. Being intimate with our Father, knowing His voice and being familiar with His ways will automatically bring life and blessing to those around us. Hungry hearts are contagious and cause others to hunger too – and God always responds to the hungry heart.

3. Be a Person of Integrity

Ladies, be true to yourselves. It is so essential that we are real and honest in what we present to others. It can be tempting, especially in the initial stages of friendship, to be what we think the other person needs, or wants, or would prefer. This type of compromise will result in superficial friendship and inevitably become rooted again in *self* rather than in Christ. We need to enjoy being who we are and recognize that Christ has placed within us unique qualities that others need and will appreciate. The longer we walk in pretence in our relationships, the tougher it becomes to let the *real us* show. The more open and transparent we are, the more others will be drawn to us.

Let me offer a word of caution here, though. We must guard who we let into our intimate world. There are different levels of friendship and we need to be wise in who we share the intimate details of our lives with. I have many friends and am a friend to many, but only a handful of people have permission to enter my private world. It would be foolish to entrust my heart to anyone and everyone. The friendships I draw from in a spiritual sense are with those who are walking in the same direction, carrying a similar heart and marching to the same drumbeat. These friendships build me up, hold me to account and enrich my life. They are precious but they are few. We cannot walk on this level with everyone.

> Do not be so deceived and misled! Evil companionships (communion, associations) corrupt and deprave good manners and morals and character.
>
> *(1 Corinthians 15:33, AMPLIFIED BIBLE)*

Hear my heart: I know we are to have a love for the lost but these are not necessarily the relationships we will be able to draw from to enrich our *spiritual* lives. While we can enjoy varying degrees of friendship with those who do not know Jesus, there is a limitation as to what they can give us as far as our spiritual well-being is concerned. We need to make sure that those we give permission to speak into our lives are a good influence on our characters and have the same Christ-centred foundations. Jesus had twelve close friends with whom He shared His private world, while also having a heart that loved, valued and accepted *all* humankind.

4. Be a Pursuer of People

We are His representatives here on the earth, His hands and His feet. We are a visual demonstration of the love of Christ to those around us. "We are the community through which the world sees Jesus." Because of this, I am confident that He will give us everything we need to touch hearts and lives.

As friends, we want to be "life-bringers" not "life-drainers". When we are absorbed in self we think like this: "No one ever calls *me*. No one ever invites *me* out for coffee. No one wants *me!*" We gradually become offended by those around us, making us even harder to love and reach out to. No one wants to spend time with someone like this. You know the kind of person I'm talking about? They walk into a room and you busy yourself quickly in another conversation to avoid having to talk to them! They suck you dry and leave you feeling miserable. You make sure you don't give them any eye contact and hope they haven't noticed you.

Instead of asking the question, "What can you give *me*?" we need to ask, "How can I be a blessing to *you*?" We need to be confident in the knowledge that we belong to our Father and that He will never let us go.

As mature daughters of the King it is necessary to pursue others, to go after them and seek them out. Do you consider yourself to be a pursuer of people? Although there are natural pursuers and those who prefer to wait to be found, I believe that each one of us has a responsibility to reach out and build friendship. It may not feel comfortable but the more we do it, the easier it will become. To pursue means not giving up at the first hurdle; setting aside time and not just having good intentions. It means pressing through any resistance or rejection we may experience and taking the initiative for the healthiness of the relationship.

We need to learn how to connect with others on a heart level. This can be particularly challenging for those of us who have wrestled with feelings of rejection in the past and why, therefore, knowing who we are and to whom we belong is so essential. Look at how Christ has so relentlessly pursued us... even at our most hardened and furthest point. He sought us out when we were at our most broken and vulnerable: "You did not choose Me but I chose you..." (John 15:16, NASB); "Come away with me, my lover" (see Song of Songs 2:10–13). This is the cry of His heart.

We need to be able to engage with other people in vulnerability and humility. Others will only open up to us if we are willing to be honest and transparent with our own lives. I am not suggesting that we bear all – we must be wise but a measure of openness is essential if the relationship is to take on any depth of meaning. Both time and patience are needed in order to see development and growth take place in our friendships. We must learn to be flexible, able to respond differently depending on the individual and where they are in their own journey.

There is One who has gone before us and modelled the life of a pursuer. He went after and sought out His twelve 2,000 years ago and today we are passionately pursued by Him, Jesus Christ, the Lover of our souls. He chose us before the foundation of the world.

> Blessed be the God and Father of our Lord Jesus Christ, who has blessed us with every spiritual blessing in the heavenly places in Christ, *just as He chose us in Him* before the foundation of the world, that we would be holy and blameless before Him. *In love He predestined us to adoption as sons* through Jesus Christ to Himself, according to the kind intention of His will...
>
> *(Ephesians 1:3–5, NASB, my italics)*

You did not choose Me but I chose you...

(John 15:16, NASB)

He *chose* us and set the example for us to go after and pursue others. We, through the revelation of all that Christ has done in and through us, are able to reach out and extend hearts that are safe and secure. This speaks volumes to those still in a place of brokenness and loneliness. As we are set free to give ourselves away, willingly and extravagantly, His love is released to flow through us into the lives of others.

5. Be Loyal and Trustworthy

There is nothing more reassuring than the knowledge that those with whom we share our hearts can be trusted and relied upon. If we are to expect any level of relationship to be built with another person, there has to be a measure of trust between us. Trust is something that can only really be proved over time, and it is a vital ingredient in meaningful relationships. In one sense, we do not know when we embark on a friendship whether the person will prove trustworthy. There is an initial stepping out, a risking of something that requires courage in order for trust to be built between friends. It is in the testing times that we really discover the true loyalty and dependability of those close to us. It is in the seasons when we entrust a piece of our hearts and see how tenderly others handle it that trust is developed. It is those who have walked a road with us who have held us up in the tough times and stuck by us through life's storms that we count as true friends indeed.

Possibly one of the most damaging things to trust can be a breaking of confidence and, as daughters of the King, we must be faithful in the way we handle the personal lives of others. I have met people who have been so damaged in this area that they are now unable to let anyone into their private world for fear of being mistreated or abused. This leads to loneliness and isolation, the very thing God declared at the beginning of creation was *not good*. This actually results in us becoming dysfunctional, and God's plan and purpose for our lives can be put in jeopardy. We are unable to find inner peace and contentment, because we are living life contrary to the perfect will of God. Where there has been a breakdown of trust, forgiveness is essential if we are ever to experience meaningful friendships again. If we have broken others' confidence we must ask their forgiveness and if we are the ones who have been hurt, forgiveness will be the only way to our healing and freedom. Communication is another essential part of the restoration process. Despite feeling hurt and disappointed, we must find the courage to bring it into the light and tell the person exactly how we are feeling. When these feelings and emotions are kept hidden they do not go away as we might hope but grow and fester like a great cancer within. Only when Christ comes in to heal and restore us are we once again enabled to reach out and begin to trust. However much hurt, pain or disappointment we may suffer at the hands of others, I believe that in Christ we have everything we need to walk in wholeness and freedom. It is not what happens to you but how you respond.

No matter how sore or tender our hearts may be right now, in Christ we can find healing and restoration; indeed, He is the only one who can heal a broken heart.

6. Be Inclusive – Not Exclusive

Jesus had an incredible gift of making others welcome and drawing in those who would naturally shrink back and live life on the fringes. There are numerous examples in the Bible where we can see He made a point of seeking out and spending time with society's outcasts and nobodies. He went to tea with a tax collector, received an anointing of perfume from a prostitute, invited the little children to come to Him, and asked a Samaritan woman for a drink, knowing that only He could give her living water.

It fascinates me to watch the different groups of mums that gather together at the school gates in those moments before the children all come racing out of their classes. There are the "Glamour Girls" who never seem to have a hair out of place, even in the most extreme weather conditions. Theirs are the umbrellas that somehow do not get blown inside out, however strong the gales. Their make-up is beautifully applied, their outfits perfectly co-ordinated and they walk steadily on the tiniest of heels. Then there are the "Fitness Fanatics" who arrive in sparkling white trainers and jogging attire, water bottles in hand and iPods strapped to their arms. The "Working Mums" are slightly harder to spot, especially if they are running late and don't have the time to actually stop the car before their children jump out! What about the "Fag Ash Lils" who have an abundance of kids, a steady supply of cigarettes that only ever get half-smoked and probably the kindest hearts of all?

If you have children, the whole "school gate" experience can be quite daunting, and you can stand there wondering where you fit in. The challenge for us, as Christians, is to ensure that in spite of our personal preferences, we are welcoming and inclusive to every member of society. When someone walks into our Sunday morning celebrations, do we look away and pretend that we have not noticed them arrive, or are we the first hand to be extended towards them? Do we go out of our way to make others feel welcome, or do we just stick to our little friendship circle and exclude those on the outside? Let us guard against being cliquey and exclusive and enjoy being secure to the point where we are able to welcome the stranger and the outsider.

As we continue on our journey to wholeness, our hearts are enlarged and we are able to reach out and love unreservedly. As daughters of the King, we carry in our hearts a love that can literally transform someone's world.

So, to conclude, friendship is a precious gift. First and foremost we have been called friends of God, and He longs to establish this unique relationship with each one of us. Only from the place of knowing who we are and to whom we belong can we truly be a friend and enjoy those who have been entrusted to us. Dying to self is the beginning of true freedom and, as we lay aside our selfish motives, we can begin to be a blessing and, indeed, be greatly blessed!

NOTE

1 Matthew Henry, *Matthew Henry's Commentary on the Whole Bible*, Nashville, Tennessee: Thomas Nelson Publishers, 2000.

2 www.thefreedictionary.com

4

Get Rid of That Stinking Thinking!
Breaking Wrong Mindsets

by Hazel

We can't solve problems by using the same kind of thinking we used when we created them.

Albert Einstein

Do not conform any longer to the pattern of this world, but be transformed by the renewing of your mind.

(Romans 12:2, NIV).

I realize more and more that my mindset and ways of thinking are sometimes seriously wonky! So often what I have taken on board as I have walked life's path and allowed to become *truth* in my life is actually rubbish. I need the power of Christ to come and bring about a transformation of the mind that leads me to green pastures, grace and freedom. As a little girl, I can remember trying so hard to be good. I would often wake up, especially on a Sunday, and whisper to myself, "Today I am going to try to be good *all* day." And try I would. From helping with chores, to having a thankful heart, to tidying my sister's room, to reading my Bible, to endeavouring to be pure and holy, I would give my all. But I can count on one hand the times I managed it; I spent the majority of my time feeling a total disappointment to both God and myself. Somehow, my perception of God and how I was able to please Him became totally warped.

Look at this definition of a mindset: "A fixed mental attitude or disposition that predetermines a person's responses to and interpretations of situations."[1]

I think my "fixed mental attitude" concerning God was rather crooked to say the least. But as I grew up, it was not only the way I saw God that became negative. Our mindsets are primarily developed in our formative years when we are too young to discern the difference between truth and error. It is only in later years that we learn to filter input from peers, colleagues, authority figures and media influences. Mindsets are established through people of influence, such as teachers, parents and guardians.

One of the greatest negative influences in my life was my primary school teacher. She was an older lady and everyone was terrified of her. She took a great dislike to me and made it very clear that I was a total disappointment to her. Any mistakes I made in her class were exposed publicly where she seemed to take delight in using my shortcomings as an opportunity to teach the rest of the class how *not* to do it. I recall a time when we had been doing potato printing in the afternoon. Her classroom was the only one in the school that had a carpet and she was very protective over it. It was time to clear away and she asked me to put the potatoes and dirty newspaper in the bin. I gathered the mess up and headed for the bin but unfortunately I tripped over someone's bag on the way and sent the potatoes flying all over her precious carpet. Needless to say she exploded. She made me stand on a chair while she announced to the class the extent of my clumsiness. She then pulled up my skirt, slapped my legs and sent me home, saying she did not want to see my face again for a very long time. My interpretation of the situation was that I was indeed very clumsy and a complete waste of space. From then on, I felt the need to apologize for my existence.

Perhaps the strongest influence comes via the generational line. It is from here that we adopt ways of thinking that have possibly been present in our parents, grandparents, great-grandparents and so on. Mindsets passed down through the generations become firmly set in our lives due to the number of years we spend in the family home, constantly exposed to those ways of thinking. The Bible commands us to renew our minds, implying that there are some wrong thought patterns that we need to identify and change. Of course, there are many mindsets that are good and positive; think of all the good habits that we developed as children and young adults. However, we need to break all the ungodly mindsets in order to live in the freedom that Christ died to bring us.

> It was for freedom that Christ set us free; therefore keep standing firm and do not be subject again to a yoke of slavery.
>
> (Galatians 5:1, NASB)

Christ died in order that we might live in the fullness of His perfect will and purposes for our lives. The work that

He carried out on the cross was a total and complete work that accomplished everything necessary for us to live an abundant life. Our sins are forgiven! Our shame is taken away and we have been cleansed from all unrighteousness! We have His promises to cling to and His Holy Spirit to empower us to live in victory on a daily basis. In order to expose our ungodly mindsets, we must first consider what a renewed mind looks like. Ask yourself the following questions:

1. Who do I think God is?

2. Who do I think I am?

3. What should a daughter of the King of kings be like?

1. Who do I think God is?

What does God look like from where you are sitting? Does God like you? Is He kind? Does He care? So many Christians that I have talked to have a warped and twisted perception of God but His Word tells us that He is "slow to anger, abounding in love" (Psalm 103:8, NIV). It also states that His "mercies ... are new every morning" (Lamentations 3:22–23, NKJV). The essence of God's character is love. This means that He *always* does the best in *every* situation. The Word is overflowing with truth concerning the nature and character of God and, as we read it, we discover that He is good and kind, caring and full of compassion. His love is always searching for a way to rescue us and His arms are always willing to embrace us. So why do we hide? Why, so often, is His presence the last place we run to in a crisis? Maybe it is because we feel so ashamed and fear that we are a disappointment to Him, that we have let Him down. But our sin and our shortcomings are no surprise to Him, are they? We need to break these mindsets with the truth of God's Word so that the lies do not erect an unnecessary barrier between us and God.

Over the past few years, God has shown me that there has been a great, fat lie buried deep in the foundations of my thinking. If you had asked me about God's character, I would have told you all the truth that is stated in His Word but deep inside, I did not believe that He was kind, or good, or that He really loved me. Recently, I have read the much-talked about book *The Shack* by William Young. It had a profound effect on me and, not long after reading it, I saw a short interview with him on YouTube. He was sharing his heart in writing the book, explaining that he had written it for his children. He went on to say how he was a pastor's kid and how he had met many other pastors' kids over the years who seemed to have fallen into two categories – those who had rebelled as a result of their upbringing, and those who lived under legalism. As I look back over my life, I see that I have done both – rebelled against the mean God I did not like or understand, as well as lived under law and not grace to the point where I was virtually suffocated. To be transformed by the renewing of our minds means to take our misunderstandings of who God is and what he looks like, and bring them in line with the truth of His Word. As I have realigned my thinking with Truth, I have been, and continue to be, transformed. It is so exciting and liberating to discover that my God is good and kind in every situation I face.

We are His vessels, created to carry His glory to the world. The enemy is a thief and a destroyer (John 10:10) and he will do all he can to attempt to break the vessel and convince us that we are in no state to carry the glory of our

King to a broken world. God's Word says, "He who is in you is greater than he who is in the world" (1 John 4:4, NKJV).

2. Who do I think I am?

Have we ever been guilty of believing that we are not lovable, we have no gifts or abilities, or that we have nothing of significance to offer?

On a personal note, I recognize that the experiences I encountered with my primary school teacher played a significant part in moulding my thinking that I was a disappointment to others. I genuinely believed that the world was better off without me getting in the way, and this fundamental lie impacted many of my close relationships. For some time I even thought that Neil and my children would be better off without me! This was a very secret thought, not one I voiced out loud, but a few years ago some friends were praying for me and one of them had a word of knowledge. He said to me, "Hazel, do you ever think that Neil and the kids would be better off without you?" My jaw hit the ground. I felt deeply ashamed and embarrassed but God set me free that day from living under a terrible lie, the seeds of which had been sown years previously.

Genesis 1 explains that we are created in His image (Genesis 1:26). In the same way that creation shouts of His beauty and His majesty, we too have been created to reflect and radiate His beauty and His glory. He has placed within men and women different attributes of His character, that together we can accurately reflect, represent and reproduce His nature. This means that we have a loving Maker who gives us worth and significance; we have all been given gifts, abilities and unique qualities that we can use for His glory. The truth is, we have a vital role to play. The stage is set and we have a part in life that no one else can perform; serving God's purpose in our generation.

3. What should a daughter of the King of kings be like?

History and culture have influenced our mindsets on how women are expected to behave and what they can and cannot do. What boxes do we place around ourselves that God never intended us to be restricted by? This is a very sensitive issue and one that has caused much heartache over the years. The Word of God once again has to be our standard. Ephesians 5:21–22 states: "… submitting to one another in the fear of God. Wives, submit to your own husbands, as to the Lord" (NKJV). The godly order of male headship and female submission brings freedom, security and safety when applied and understood in a truly biblical way. Headship is not domination or control, and submission is not subservience or being controlled. The word "submit" means "to arrange yourself under". This implies respect and a voluntary choosing to follow someone's lead. This principle applies in a husband/wife context and in a church leadership context. A husband or a leader should lead the individual (justly and lovingly) and not overrule the individual (like a dictator). When we are able to apply this biblical principle correctly, we are free from any rebellious Feminist agenda. It has astounded me to see the freedom and release that this has brought to ladies within Jubilee Church as they have embraced the principle. One lady shared with me recently, with tears in her eyes, of the transformation that has taken place in her marriage as a direct result of applying it. Her husband is now released to lead in a godly way and she is experiencing a new measure

70

of freedom and security. A daughter of the King is: gentle, loving, kind, tender, compassionate; and at the same time: confident, secure in her identity, self-assured and engaged in her gifting and destiny.

As you read this, you may realize that you follow wrong mindsets, or that some parts of your thinking are not in line with the truth of His Word. Good news! God has given us everything needed to expel the destructive, negative thought patterns and replace them with His life-giving ways of thinking.

Let me share with you some of the wrong mindsets I inherited as I grew up. Some were a result of my wrong perceptions, some were a result of years of church tradition and others were a result of my agreement with the lies of the enemy. Although this is subjective, I think it worth mentioning because I have encountered many other ladies, especially from churches in the UK, who share similar wrong mindsets.

When I look back over the years, I can see clearly how the enemy has sought to place yokes upon women's shoulders that we were never created to carry. Growing up all my life in "the church" brought with it many challenges, and although today I thank God for my Christian heritage, there has been significant baggage that has hindered and hampered my journey along the way. I cannot go any further in my writing without honouring my parents, who have passed down such godly thinking, despite the fact that they too were subject to the same wrong mindsets. Their love and passion for the King of kings, their unrelenting pursuit of truth and their selfless example of kingdom living are a constant inspiration to me.

Living under law rather than grace is indeed a heavy yoke to bear and I felt stifled and wearied by it. There were two ungodly mindsets that I think I took on board during my years in the church and I praise God that in His great mercy He has brought me out from both of them. On the one hand, there was a sense of worthlessness and oppression that I came under. I felt invisible and I remember crying out on numerous occasions, "There must be more than this!" I was not alone in this cry and there were a number of us who wanted so much more than what we had experienced. But we did not know what it was or what it looked like.

The cry of our hearts, "There must be more than this!" was heard not only by our Father, but also by our enemy. In a place of oppression and pain, Satan crept in and began to fuel the fire. He stoked and he provoked us. There was an outcry that rang out from women's hearts and they rose up from the dust with much to prove. The mindset shifted over time from one of oppression and worthlessness to one that said, "Whatever the men can do, we can do too." Rebellion took a hold of hearts and distorted again our original design. We became aggressive and deeply defensive. Ministries were set up to compete with rather than complement that which already existed. An undermining of leadership and authority developed and an ungodly spirit lay behind many of the motivations of our hearts. As a result of that time, I lived for many years feeling worthless and insignificant. I walked for many years with bitterness and a hardness of heart. I have had to forgive those who knew no better but who caused deep wounds in my soul.

For so many years, this perception of church caused it to be a place of bondage and confusion to me. The shame and the guilt I carried were at times almost unbearable. You see, I knew that Christ was passionate about His church! For ten years I was in full-time ministry and yet deep inside I wondered why. Of course, no one ever knew! I had learned, like countless others, to play my part and to do what was right. I gave very little attention to the ache, the cry in my heart, because I was so utterly ashamed of how I really felt. I was trapped, knowing that He loved His bride and therefore I had to serve the church – yet on the inside I despised it. For more than thirty years, church was just a building to me. It was a place of law and not grace; a place of rules and traditions. By nature I wanted to please – I think many of us do. I wanted to please my Jesus but lived under a constant sense of failure, not being good enough or able to sustain my good intentions. I wanted other Christians to see me as a "good Christian girl" and I perfected the role. But inside, I was crumbling. I swung from being *really, really good* to being *really, really bad* and both extremes left me feeling sick in the very pit of my stomach. "God! There must be more than this!"

It has only been in the last six years or so that I have had a revelation that has totally transformed me. The error came firstly in my wrong mindset of "church" and secondly in how I, as a woman, fitted into it. Jesus taught a radical kingdom message but our often tainted perspectives add a number of false "gospels" to the one that Jesus brought. These "gospels" contain elements of the truth wrapped in a lie. There is the "gospel of salvation" and the "gospel of the church". These are wrong mindsets that bring bondage into our lives and are present when God's order is absent. There is one true gospel that Jesus taught, the *gospel of the kingdom*. It is a message of good news, a life-changing message of hope. Let us have a brief look at these "gospels".

"Gospel of Salvation"

Jesus came to this earth so that we – humankind – could be reconciled with our heavenly Father. What a thought! Salvation is one of the key principles that the Christian Faith is built on and it is therefore very important that as the bride of Christ we understand the fullness of this truth. Salvation *is* good news. However, in our desperation to "get people saved" I do not believe the church has always accurately presented the good news of salvation to people.

I am sure many of us can remember a time when many people "got saved" motivated purely by fear of the alternative – an eternity burning in hell! Many evangelical crusaders cried, "Turn or burn!" as they welcomed terrified sinners with open arms onto their podiums. Good news? I think not! Romans 2:4 says, "Or do you despise the riches of His kindness, and the forbearance and long-suffering, not knowing that the kindness of God leads you to repentance?" (MKJV).

Then there was the time when many Christians responded to a message that said, "Come to Jesus and you'll be saved from your sins. Come to Jesus and receive eternal life. Jesus is the door to salvation." They prayed the sinners' prayer, experienced the euphoria of the moment – but then either disappeared within six months, or settled down to a mediocre, seat-filling, "feed me" form of Christianity.

The weakness has been in the presentation of the gospel message. The full truth is that we must acknowledge Him as *Lord* as well as *saviour* in our lives – many of us only got the saviour part. Picture yourself sitting on the throne (chair) of your life. When we receive Jesus as saviour, we are still firmly seated, with Jesus next to us. Acknowledging His Lordship involves us actively removing ourselves,

74

placing Jesus on the throne of our lives and kneeling at His feet, ready to obey. In doing this, we take the first step in *dying to self*. I believe that many who were saved without the full understanding that there is a cost involved, became seriously disillusioned because they were not presented with a complete gospel message. Salvation is more than merely praying the sinner's prayer; it is a life transformed.

"Gospel of the Church"

Jesus is passionate about His church but He never made the church the centre of His teaching. When we make church our focus, we can end up as slaves serving an institution that no longer breathes life and no longer reflects the Life-Giver.

The Greek word for "church" is *ekklesia* – the *called out ones*. Isn't that awesome? That is you and I, living people – not an institution, or a stuffy building! We have been called out from that place of darkness into His marvellous light. Once we were not a people – but now we are the people of God (1 Peter 2:9–10)! The "gospel" of the church builds walls and rivalries between different churches as people build their own empires, focusing on traditions and methodology; a far cry from Jesus' prayer 'that they may be one' (John 17:22).

Jesus' message was simple: Follow me! He never called meetings, or set up a building fund; He simply travelled from village to village, teaching and feeding those who were hungry and healing the sick. I wonder what He thinks about this institution we have created?

Gospel of the Kingdom

Jesus said, "I am the door" (John 10:9, NASB), implying that a door leads somewhere. Jesus opens up a way for us into the kingdom of God and the only way into this kingdom is through the door. Salvation is the very first step; a step that takes us to the door. I often feel amazed and perplexed when I see so many people who "get saved" and then spend the rest of their lives standing in the doorway, not realizing that the kingdom is where they are meant to be!

> But seek first the kingdom of God and His righteousness; and all these things shall be added to you.
>
> *(Matthew 6:33, MKJV)*

During His earthly ministry, Jesus proclaimed the kingdom of God, of which the church is also a significant part. Jesus taught about radically changing our self-centred lives through understanding and applying God's order. The kingdom of God operates from the top down, with the King issuing His commands. We are transformed from the inside out, choosing to allow Jesus' transforming power to change our hearts. Jesus proclaimed that God's kingdom was not a physical place but that it existed in the hearts of men and women wherever His rule and reign operates.

> Nor shall they say, Lo here! or, behold, there! For behold, the kingdom of God is in your midst.
>
> *(Luke 17:21, MKJV)*

When we make the kingdom of God our focus, petty rivalries, jealousies and disagreements disappear and leave an attitude of, "Unless *your* church is succeeding, we are failing"! Rules, regulations and structures of men fade, leaving a living organism ready to accept the rule and reign of God. Godly order is established in our lives, churches, towns and cities. We can then pray a blessing: "your kingdom come, your will be done on earth as it is in heaven" (Matthew 6:10, NIV). Where kingdom is the focus, God's will is done and His rule and reign are established on the earth. (We will share on this in far greater detail in chapter 8).

Often we are unaware of our wrong mindsets and learn to "accept" the way we are, assuming that nothing can be done to alter it. We have our limitations, our "areas of defeat", and over time we possibly resign ourselves to the fact that "this is as good as it gets for me"! This is the place in which the enemy wants us to remain.

In order to break these wrong mindsets, we must consider two important areas: truth and deception, and the power of agreement.

Truth and Deception

In John 8:31–32, Jesus says, "Then Jesus said to the Jews who believed on Him, If you continue in My Word, you are My disciples indeed. And you shall know the *truth*, and the *truth* shall make you free" (MKJV, my italics). Jesus was speaking to His disciples in the context of them actively following and applying His teaching, leading them to freedom. So what is the truth? I realize more and more that there is *my* truth, *your* truth and the *actual* truth. So often what we perceive to be the whole truth is not accurate or complete. So, what is our knowledge and understanding of the truth? Let's look at the following three statements:

- All that I have learned is all that I know.

- All that I have learned is not all there is to know.

- All that I know is not necessarily so.

Imagine our minds as filing cabinets in which we have truth drawers and lie drawers. We seek to filter all the information during our lives and try to neatly classify everything as true or false. The reality is that all of us misinterpret some truth as lies and some lies as truth. The consequence is that we end up with lies in our truth drawer and truths in our lie drawer. The Holy Spirit seeks to rectify this situation.

The first two statements imply that we are all a sum of our experiences so far, and most of us would admit to not having a complete and perfect knowledge of everything! The third statement recognizes that some of the information we have filed in our truth drawer is actually not true but a lie.

Most spiritual warfare takes place in the area of our minds and it is in this place that the enemy seeks to distort and counterfeit God's sovereign truth with his lies and deceptions. The enemy rejoices when we accept lies into our truth drawer.

> For though we walk in the flesh, we do not war according to the flesh. For the weapons of our warfare are not carnal but mighty in God for pulling down strongholds, casting down arguments and every high thing that exalts itself against the knowledge of God, bringing every thought into captivity to the obedience of Christ...
>
> (2 Corinthians 10:3–5, NKJV, *my italics*)

In his book, *Spiritual Warfare*, Dean Sherman says the following:

> However, in 2 Corinthians, *strongholds* does not refer to massive complex systems, human or demonic. Here it refers to the *strongholds of the mind*. These strongholds are castles in the air, built up in our minds through wrong thinking – through unbelieving, depressed, fearful and negative thinking.[2]

These mental strongholds must be cast down through an active attitude of aggression in the spiritual realm. Our struggle is not against flesh and blood and our efforts must be directed against the real enemy in the battlefield of the mind. We need to be careful of what we store in our truth drawer and root out the lies that are already there. We must learn to be quick in taking thoughts captive, those thoughts that are not in line with the truth of God's Word. This is why it is so vital that we know and meditate upon His Word. We cannot afford to be apathetic or half-hearted in this area. How often, for example, have we lived under a mindset that suggests "I will never be free from my guilt"? What a lie! What does the Word say on this matter? 1 John 1:9: "If we confess our sins, He is faithful and righteous to forgive us our sins and to *cleanse* us from all unrighteousness" (NASB, my italics). Through the redeeming blood of Christ we are counted worthy!

A few years ago, I was leading a meeting with Heather with other leaders' wives from the Maidstone area. I was excited about what God was going to do and was feeling quite comfortable and at peace about the evening. But then two ladies walked in who I found particularly intimidating. Suddenly I was shaking in my boots and ready to run from the room in fear. The Word says, "God has not given us a spirit of fear, but of power and of love and of a sound mind" (2 Timothy 1:7, NKJV). I spoke this Scripture under my breath and rebuked a spirit of intimidation. The outcome was an immediate sense of peace and the fear left me. As we grow in our love and knowledge of His Word, we can become quick and effective in identifying and resisting wrong mindsets from being established in our thinking. We need to be alert to every thought that sets itself up against the truth of His Word, actively resisting it, and we need to allow the Holy Spirit to reveal to us those areas in our lives where we are living under wrong mindsets. Spiritual warfare is *active*. There is no room for passivity. If you are a timid, passive person, find someone to stand with you and provoke you to war! 2 Timothy 1:7 underlines that the Spirit we have received is not one that makes us timid and, despite our personality type, we can be empowered to fight and overcome.

The Power of Agreement

Often the starting point on the slippery slope to establishing wrong mindsets is in the fact that we allow ourselves to *agree* with the lies that our enemy fires at us. There is great power in agreement; power that operates in both a positive and a negative context.

In Matthew 18:19, Jesus says, "Again, I tell you that if two of you on earth *agree* about anything you ask for, it will be done for you by my Father in heaven" (NIV, my italics). Jesus refused to *agree* with the accusations that Satan threw at Him in the wilderness, giving him no foothold or point of access. When we begin to agree with the subtle whisperings of the deceiver, we become far more vulnerable and quickly descend into a place of captivity. Jesus' way of dealing with the tempter was to face him head-on, directly, giving no room for the accusation to take hold or fester in His thinking. He confronted the enemy, out loud, with authority and using the Word of God. We need to take heed of His example to us and no longer entertain the lies and false accusations. It is important to ask ourselves this question: "Do I find myself agreeing with the accusations of the enemy?" If so, we must repent and stop it! He is a liar and the father of all lies (John 8:44), so why are we even listening? We need to confront our enemy, declaring the truth of God's Word, using the authority that is ours in Christ. Be quick and active to resist him and "… he *will* flee from you" (James 4:7, NIV, my italics).

The last few years have been quite a journey for me as I have begun to identify, through the Spirit, those places where I have lived in bondage, believing things to be the "truth" when, in actual fact, they were far from it. I think there are many mindsets in which we operate that need to be broken in order for us to enter into the freedom that should be ours. What lies are we believing now that are contrary to the Word of God? Take stock of your life and ask the Holy Spirit to highlight any thought patterns that are destructive or out of line with His Word.

Let me finish my part of the story. After living under the "gospel of the church" for so long, and becoming totally disillusioned with it, I was almost at breaking point. I hit a crisis and honestly wondered if my church-going days were over. It was during this season in my life that God led Neil and I to join the family at Jubilee Church and I am so grateful to Him for the body He has placed us in here. Our Senior Pastor, Michael Puffett, often says "Constant change is here to stay" and I have learnt to really love the fact that there is no such thing as "a normal Sunday morning celebration". Our times together are very unpredictable; full of life, intimacy, fun and laughter, thus preventing us from becoming stuck in a rut. In the Spirit, we need to be continually looking out for the next wave to leap upon (but, of course, the foundation of His truth is unchanging). So often God does something new and fresh but we hold onto it for so long that it becomes stale and stagnant.

> Forget the former things;
> do not dwell on the past.
> See, I am doing a new thing!
> ... do you not perceive it?
>
> *(Isaiah 43:18–19, NIV)*

The Lord wants us to be continually straining ahead – looking forward to the next new thing. He is a God of new beginnings, His creative juices do not dry up and He is always on the move.

God has realigned my thinking and understanding of church. I love His house now! I am free of the shame and guilt of the past. I see now that much of what I struggled with and fought against were the very things that Christ resisted. The group of people that He opposed the most were the religious leaders of His day. He saw right through their spiritual projections, their hypocrisy and their legalism. He saw clearly how these religious leaders placed a yoke upon the people's shoulders that they should never have had to carry.

> ... for they bind heavy burdens, hard to bear, and lay them on men's shoulders; but they themselves will not move them with one of their fingers.
>
> *(Matthew 23:4, NKJV)*

Are you carrying heavy burdens that others have bound to your shoulders – burdens that are not of God? Allow Him to take them from you in order that you may enter into the freedom that He died to bring you.

Sadly, in the past I wandered from the safety of my Father's embrace and made poor choices, looking for love in the wrong places, which led to much heartache and regret. A love given graciously and undeservedly is the only thing that can free us from such a lifestyle. Remember the sinful woman who entered the Pharisee's house and washed Jesus' feet with her tears and wiped them with her hair (Luke 7:36–50)? She knew she was a sinner, desperately in need of a saviour. He was the only one able to forgive her – and He extended to her a love she had never known, and did not deserve. She was forgiven much and consequently loved much. When we encounter such love, our lives are changed – for ever transformed. Only when we are healed can we begin to join the dance. As we spend time in His presence, our lives cannot fail to be changed, for the more time we spend *with* Him the more we will become *like* Him. Instead of fearing His presence, we need to run into it, allowing Him to bring about the transformation that we are so desperate for.

NOTE

1 www.thefreedictionary.com

2 Dean Sherman, *Spiritual Warfare*, Seattle, Washington: YWAM Publishing, 1995.

5

Paediatrics to Geriatrics

Our Journey to Maturity

by Heather

You've got to do your own growing, no matter how
tall your grandfather was.

Irish Proverb

We are in a season where God is calling us as
His precious daughters to enter into all that
He has prepared for us. Part of that means
imparting wisdom from our life experiences to others. We
are not all necessarily called to upfront ministry or church
leadership but we do *all* have something to contribute, a
role to play, a song to sing, a story to tell. I urge you to step
in and join the dance! Not from a place of worthlessness,
nor from a heart that is hardened and rebellious, but as
one who willingly responds to the voice of her Father. It is
time to shake off the dust and rise up from the ashes. Have
we been content with second best for too long? Maybe we

have slipped into that place of indifference, not even daring to believe that there could be more for us than this? My friend, there is so much more! It is time to break wrong mindsets (strongholds), cease our agreements with the enemy and to begin to appropriate the truth of God's Word in our lives. But take heed: If we do so, we may never be the same again!

When Jesus taught His disciples to pray, He reminded them of God's fatherhood and taught us to address Him as "*Our Father* which art in heaven..." (Matthew 6:9, KJV). He is our Dad! He loves us and we are able to relate to Him in the same way that we would a good earthly father. This means that there is not only Someone to whom we belong but One who passionately and unconditionally loves us because He created us. This is true both physically and spiritually – we all have an earthly father as well as a heavenly Father.

> I will be a Father to you, and you will be my sons and daughters...
>
> *(2 Corinthians 6:18, NIV)*

God is Someone whom we can love and trust to the point where we are prepared to lay our very lives down at His feet, knowing that He has our best interests at heart.

I pray that we never take this incredible truth for granted. Because our Father in heaven created us, He knows us intimately – both our strengths and our weaknesses. If you have any doubts in this area, may I suggest that you spend some time meditating on Psalm 139; the depth to which He knows us impacts me every time I read it. He knows the beginning from the end because He is the Alpha and the Omega (Revelation 1:8). He has a plan for our lives

(Jeremiah 29:11), part of which is to mature us and grow us to become more Christ-like.

It breaks my heart that there are so many dads who have let their children down in their role as father. They have caused untold damage to their children, often because good fatherhood was never modelled to them when they were growing up. I believe the lack of fathering we see in society today has been a tool that Satan has used to hinder, and sometimes even completely destroy, our ability to relate to and understand the role of God as our heavenly Father.

One of the misconceptions of God that I have witnessed is where God is seen as a tyrant. We all know that it can be extremely difficult to please a tyrant and so people who see God in this way struggle to feel worthy, loved and accepted. They spend much of their time striving; doing as many good works as possible in order to appease God.

There are also those who see God as "Father Christmas"; their expectations are that He needs to be attentive to their every whim and fancy. They feel terribly let down if for some reason God decides not to respond to the entire shopping list that they have brought before Him.

Or what about those who feel that God just cannot be trusted? They have been so let down by their own father that they end up wearing glasses of mistrust through which they interpret everything.

And then there are those who have grown up with an "absent" father. Is Father God really interested in them as individuals and are they really worthy of His time and affection?

A good book that has been written on this subject is The Father Heart of God by Floyd McClung, where he identifies the fact that the term "father" so often provokes a negative response. If you struggle to relate to God as your father because of a warped perception of fatherhood, then I recommend that you read this book and find someone to pray through any hurts and unforgiveness that you may still be carrying from your childhood.

God, because of His great love for us and a desire for us to truly see Him as Dad, sent Jesus to reveal the Father to us. John recorded a powerful conversation that Jesus had with Philip:

> Philip said, "Lord, show us the Father and that will be enough for us." Jesus answered: "Don't you know me, Philip, even after I have been among you such a long time? *Anyone who has seen me has seen the Father*. How can you say, 'Show us the Father'?"
>
> *(John 14:8–9, NIV, my italics)*

We are on a journey; a process in which we experience very distinct seasons in our lives. About 700 years before Jesus was even born, Isaiah's prophecy describes the process from childhood to adulthood as follows:

> For unto us a *Child* is born,
> Unto us a *Son* is given,
> And the government will be upon His shoulder.
> And His name will be called
> Wonderful, Counselor, Mighty God,
> *Everlasting Father*, Prince of Peace.
>
> *(Isaiah 9:6, NKJV, my italics)*

I find it is important to note that God is not gender specific when He refers to us as "sons".

> You are *all* sons of God through faith in Christ Jesus, for *all* of you who were baptized into Christ have

clothed yourselves with Christ. There is neither Jew nor Greek, slave nor free, male nor female, for you are *all* one in Christ Jesus. If you belong to Christ, then you are Abraham's seed, and heirs according to the promise.

(Galatians 3:26–29, NIV, *my italics*)

For if you live according to the flesh you will die; but if by the Spirit you put to death the deeds of the body, you will live. For *as many* as are led by the Spirit of God, *these* are sons of God.

(Romans 8:13–14, NKJV, *my italics*)

The physical growth stages that we experience in life accurately mirror the way that we grow and mature spiritually. In the following Scripture, we can clearly see the different stages of development on our journey to maturity:

I write to you, dear *children*, because your sins have been forgiven on account of his name. I write to you, *fathers*, because you have known him who is from the beginning. I write to you, *young men*, because you have overcome the evil one. I write to you, dear *children*, because you have known the Father. I write to you, *fathers*, because you have known him who is from the beginning. I write to you, *young men*, because you are strong, and the word of God lives in you, and you have overcome the evil one.

(1 John 2:12–14, NIV, *my italics*)

For me, a steep learning curve was realizing that these different stages of maturity usually have nothing to do with our physical age. I have known of men and women who have been Christians for many years, yet the fruit of their lives show very little maturity. Alternatively, I have known of men and women in their twenties who have matured to the place where they are actively fathering their own spiritual sons and daughters. In which stage of maturity do you most identify yourself? The goal for each one of us should be to reach that place of spiritual maturity where we can enjoy meat and not just the milk.

1. Baby

Firstly, there is the stage where we are babies, the time when we first accept Jesus as saviour in our lives. It is a time when we understand that our sins have been forgiven and that we are a "new creation" (2 Corinthians 5:17).

> Therefore, rid yourselves of all malice and all deceit, hypocrisy, envy, and slander of every kind. Like newborn babies, crave pure spiritual milk, so that by it you may grow up in your salvation, now that you have tasted that the Lord is good.
>
> *(1 Peter 2:1–3, NIV)*

The Greek word for this stage is *nepios* which reminds me of one who is in nappies! It is during this stage that God's presence is richly manifest in our lives; He is right there – with a tangible sense of His presence, ready to help us as we conquer those initial obstacles that we face. New babies in Christ need someone walking closely by them during this season, as it is often in infancy that Satan seeks to "take us out". A lot of nurturing love, care and support are needed. Firm boundaries must be put in place to provide safety and protection; it is at this stage that a healthy, regular reading of the Word of God and learning to recognize the voice of our Father begins to develop.

The first time I heard God's voice is still so clear in my mind. Prior to this occasion, I remember feeling terribly worried that something was wrong with me as no matter how hard I listened, I heard nothing! We were sitting in a small group, praying, when suddenly I had an overwhelming sense of God's love for us. Not saying a word to rest of the group, I continued to just meditate on the love of God. A friend in the same group then said that He felt that God wanted to tell us how much He loved us. I was amazed. I had heard that too! I realized then that God had been speaking all along but I had failed to recognize that it had been His voice.

> My sheep *listen* to my voice; I know them, and they follow me.
>
> (John 10:27, NIV)

2. Young Child

> Brothers, stop thinking like *children*. In regard to evil be infants, but in your thinking be adults.
>
> (1 Corinthians 14:20, NIV)

The original Greek word used in this Scripture for "children" is *paidion*, which is the next stage of maturity in our lives. This could be compared to a young child; one who has grown up a little and maybe even picked up a few bumps and bruises along the way. It is during this stage that we sometimes have to learn things the hard way! Many times we, if we are parents, are able to see the hidden dangers when our children are exploring and trying out new things. There are times when we need to be firm and there are times, especially when dealing with a more stubborn child, that we need to let them experience certain things for themselves. Often, those of us in the "young child" stage prefer to *avoid* any obstacles that we may encounter, because we are still learning what it means to be an overcomer. It is also a season of slightly more freedom, in which we begin to carry some of the responsibility for our own growth.

I was once someone who looked to others to remove obstacles from my path. I used to really struggle in the whole area of *pushing through*. It was only after hearing a message on the woman with the issue of blood (Mark 5:25–34) and how she had to literally push her way through the crowd to get to Jesus, that I appreciated that there was an effort on my part involved. When the mountain feels too high to climb, it is so much easier to just give up! The fact that we live in an instant society that expects instant results is not helpful either. I know that the enemy is delighted when we give up – it means he has won that round. The thing I have learned that now causes me to push through is that the darkest hour is just before dawn.

There have often been times where the prospect of an evening meeting seems daunting to say the least. It was when we first started kingdom mentoring that this was such a reality for me. We meet with ladies from across the town on the first Monday of every month and, low and behold, every first Monday would leave me feeling as though I had run a marathon all day long. This was usually before we had even got to the evening meal where I often realized how much homework still needed completing, that the washing had not yet been done and that we would probably be out of bread and milk by the morning. The very last thing I felt like doing was going out to a meeting. And yet, as I learned to push through while focusing on the bigger picture, I discovered that these obstacles were merely a tactic of the enemy to prevent me from going to the meeting. The hardest meetings to get to are usually the meetings where God shows up in a mighty way; meetings definitely not to be missed!

3. Adolescent

> As obedient *children*, do not conform to the evil desires you had when you lived in ignorance. But just as he who called you is holy, so be holy in all you do...
>
> (1 Peter 1:14–15, NIV, my italics)

The original Greek word used for "children" in this passage is *teknon*, which refers to a child or children old enough to have been nurtured and moulded by wisdom. Today, we would refer to this stage as adolescence. During this stage, it is common for some Christians to feel that because they have a bit of experience and growth, they know everything! We are still learning that there is a personal cost involved and we begin to "put to death" the ways of the flesh within us (Romans 8:13). It is during this time that *teknons* are learning how to behave like a son or a daughter of the King – we are learning the *protocol of the Palace*. It is a time, however, when we can possibly become unteachable and pride can easily enter our lives. In this stage, one can be quite stubborn and even slightly rebellious. This is a good time to experience missions led by mature men and women where we can actively get involved in watching and learning under close supervision. It is important that we face challenges that have been set for us and begin to learn to rise above circumstances and emotions.

For many years, Michael and I ran the youth group at a large church in South Africa where we were dealing with some determined, passionate young adults who felt a strong desire and calling to serve God. What a pleasure! For those of you who have ever worked with this particular age group, you'll appreciate that they are not well known for tact or pretence. There was a tendency for youth leaders to water down the truth of the gospel in order to keep their young adults. "As long as they're having fun!" seemed all that mattered. Young adults are usually known to be passionate people and so our motto became "Give them something to die for!" When we prepared them for their first mission to a school hostel about four hours away, they had to learn many relevant Scriptures by heart. After our first evening of dance/drama and some sharing, they had their first uncomfortable night, sleeping on the floor of the school's squash court. They were starting to learn what it means to be "crucified with Christ and I no longer live, but Christ lives in me" (Galatians 2:20, NIV).

Even though the years have passed, we are still in contact with many of these people and they still talk about that mission trip, how much they learned, and how their lives changed as a result of someone believing in them.

4. Mature Son

This next stage, called the *huios* stage, describes the mature sons of God. This is one of the most exciting stages in the life of a Christian, because it is here that we begin to feel secure in our identity.

> For if you live according to the sinful nature, you
> will die; but if by the Spirit you put to death the
> misdeeds of the body, you will live, because those
> who are led by the Spirit of God are sons of God...
>
> *(Romans 8:13–14, NIV)*

As mature sons and daughters, we have learned to be led by the Spirit as opposed to being led by our emotions. We know the voice of our Father and are able to recognize the lies of the enemy. We know the truth of God's Word and know what it means to walk in freedom.

Jesus was acknowledged by God, after being baptized, as "His beloved Son" – *huios*. Straight after this, the Bible says He was led by the Spirit into the wilderness. As mature sons, we can be sure that there will be times of testing and even hardship that we will need to face, endure and learn to overcome. God's presence is sometimes hidden during this time and, as we walk the road through the wilderness, we need to learn to find Him as we seek Him with all our hearts (Jeremiah 29:13–14, NIV).

What, then, does a mature son or daughter of God look like?

• By now, there has been significant growth in our lives and we know and understand the importance of purpose and destiny in our lives;

• We are secure in the knowledge of who we are in Christ and therefore do not show signs of competitiveness or striving for position;

• We have an intimate relationship with our father (heavenly Father and spiritual father) and are usually beginning to walk alongside others in the kingdom in order to lead those coming behind us into a place of maturity;

- We are committed to serving the vision of the church and are able to take the initiative when things need doing. In this way, we can practically serve the body of Christ;

- It is a time when we could be released into a role of supervised leadership and try out different styles of leadership, possibly through a process of trial and error, establishing in our minds what does and does not work;

- We walk with passion and a very strong sense of loyalty towards our leadership;

- We are not easily influenced if strife or discontent enters the body of Christ;

- As mature sons and daughters we know our freedom – we are no longer a slave, but a son or daughter of the King.

There is a huge difference between being a son and being a slave. There was a season where I worked for God, my Master, out of a sense of duty. I praise God that I am now more secure in my identity and I realize that God is not impressed with what I can do for Him. I recognize that I have also changed in the whole area of my self-image. I now feel far more secure in the fact that I am valued by God and do not need to compare myself to others and their giftings. Another area where I have seen growth in my life is through the way in which I view admonition. I now see correction as a real blessing and an opportunity for growth, whereas in the past I used to feel very hurt because of my need to be right in different situations.

As I have grown and matured in these areas, I have become far more confident. These have been some of the key truths that have helped to *sift* and *shake* fear and insecurity from my life.

Romans 8:15 confirms this: "For you did not receive a

spirit that makes you a slave again to fear, but you received the Spirit of sonship. And by him we cry, "Abba, Father" (NIV).

5. Father

The final stage in our growth is when we enter this stage of fatherhood. The original Greek and Aramaic word for "father" is *pater* and *abba* which means "source" or "sustainer". This stage signifies maturity and wisdom, when Christians have learned the truth that we are *more than conquerors* (Romans 8:37) because we have passed the test and have learned to overcome. It means that reproduction has taken place. We have reproduced what God has done in our lives in the life of someone else. This is the time where God sets us apart as He places a mantle of new authority on our shoulders. We can flow in an anointing and carry influence in the lives of our spiritual sons and daughters by specifically and purposefully walking alongside them, cheering them on in their walk with the Father. Our desire is that we will see our sons and daughters go further and accomplish more than we ever could.

I really love the picture of fatherhood that Jesus painted in the parable of the prodigal (or lost) son (Luke 15:11–32) who ran off and squandered his inheritance. Jesus describes how, when the boy returned, the father – who had obviously been watching for him – could see him from a long way off. It is important to remember that this son had been living in a pig sty – can you imagine the state he was in? Jesus goes on to explain how the father ran to meet his son and how he hugged and kissed him. The father then called for a robe, ring and sandals to be placed on his son and ordered that the fattened calf be brought for the banquet to celebrate his return. This was before the boy had even been washed.

What an incredible picture of God's heart towards us. The son had done nothing to earn his father's favour and yet the love and grace lavished upon him was incredible. I continue to pray for God to increase the love in my heart for the precious sons and daughters who look to both Michael and I for spiritual parenting.

I read an incredible story originally from *The Washington Post*, recounted by Larry Kreider in his book, *The Cry for Spiritual Fathers & Mothers*.

The Washington Post reported the plight of the white rhinoceros in Pilanesberg Park, South African Game Reserve.

At least 39 of these endangered rhinos had been found slaughtered in their native habitat, and it was assumed that poachers were the killers of the remarkable beasts. However, upon closer in inspection it was discovered that all of the rhinos' valuable horns remained among the carcasses. In an effort to catch the killers, the game wardens decided to tranquilize some of the remaining animals to electronically tag and track them. Hidden video cameras were also set in strategic locations to record the evidence.

The game wardens were amazed to discover that young bull elephants were harassing the rhinos without provocation. Although unnatural for them, these teenaged elephants were chasing these white rhinos for long distances, throwing sticks at them and stomping them to death. Why were these elephants acting so violently? The answer would be found in a decision made 20 years earlier.

Because the Kruger National Park was unable to support a continuously increasing population of elephants, park officials had decided to transport some of them to the Pilanesberg Reserve. The elephants too large to transport were killed, including a significant number of mature bulls. As a result, the elephants that were guilty of killing the rhinos matured without the influence and presence of mature males. Park rangers and scientists discovered that without the older presence of mature bulls, these young male elephants were suffering from excessive testosterone and becoming increasingly violent.

To preserve the white rhino population, park officials killed five of the most aggressive young bull elephants while determining to find a suitable answer for this aberration of nature. Park rangers decided to import older bulls in order to view their influence on the remaining young males. The young bulls learned quickly that they were no match for the more mature elephants. The older bulls began to assume their place among the herd as fathers and disciplinarians.

The younger, aggressive bulls could no longer impose their unchallenged, immature bullying. Eventually the young bulls began following the older ones. It became apparent that they enjoyed these new relationships with the older, more mature males. The former lawbreakers yielded to the new discipline and returned to normal patterns of elephant behaviour. There has not been a report of any dead rhinos since the arrival of the more mature elephants.[1]

I feel a chill down my spine as I reflect upon a "fatherless" society, particularly prevalent in the UK. Even the politicians are starting to see the devastating effects that broken homes impose on our young people; where for a long time now, many children have grown up being left to their own devices.

This story sadly mirrors what happens in many churches today. The world is crying out for fathers (and mothers) and we need to rise up in the fullness of all that God has called us to. Just as a biological father walks closely beside the son he is raising, we too need to be modelling spiritual fathering to the next generation.

NOTE

1 Larry Kreider *The Cry for Spiritual Fathers & Mothers*, Dove Christian Fellowship International, 2008.

6

Keeping All Your Plates Spinning

The Importance of Managing Time

by Heather

Never get so busy doing the work of the Kingdom
that you forget who the King is.

Unknown

So many times I have driven past a graveyard and thought about the tragedy of how many unsung songs, unwritten books and unfulfilled dreams are buried there... for ever. I once heard a profound statement: "there are only two things worth leaving behind when we go to be with the Lord. One is resources; the other is spiritual sons and daughters." However, finding time to think and worry about where others are at is a real challenge. Face it, there are very few people today who are not continuously looking for ways to include a bit more "me" time in their daily, weekly or monthly regimes. How often do we feel that if we squeeze just one more thing into our agendas we'll collapse under the weight of it all? There have been many nights when, as I've reflected upon my day, I have felt as though I have been chasing my tail as I have rushed from one meeting or activity to the next.

Hazel and I have shared on many different occasions with enquiring church leaders about the mentoring programme we lead in Jubilee Church. Although these leaders are acutely aware of the deep need that their people have for more meaningful relationships, one of their main concerns seems to be that they feel their people are already too busy! It is not easy to fulfil the many demanding expectations that society places on women today. Many of us have so much to see to – husbands, children, households, careers, recreation... As Joanna Weaver so aptly puts it in her excellent book, *Having a Mary Heart in a Martha World*, "being a woman requires more stamina, more creativity, and more wisdom than I ever dreamed as a young girl."[1]

Our heavenly Father is relational to the core and this is made clear from the outset in the Word, where God said, "let *Us* make man in *Our* image" (Genesis 1:26, NASB, my italics). He was not a lone ranger; He worked alongside His Son and the Holy Spirit, creating the world. He has created you and me in His image, which means that we too are relational to the core! I believe that it is this area of our lives, our *relationships*, where we are most vulnerable to the attack of the enemy.

The enemy is out to "steal and kill and destroy" (John 10:10, NASB) our relationships with one another. He knows all too well the protection that comes through having people close by who know and love us. He uses situations where we have been hurt, often through miscommunication, to cause division in our relationships. He wants to isolate us and we need to know that he'll do all he can to keep us from developing godly friendships and thus living life to the full.

The enemy knows that "where two or three have gathered together in My name, I am there in their midst" (Matthew 18:20, NASB). How powerful is that? I literally cringe as I remember a season in my life when I was so busy doing the work of the kingdom I felt that I did not have the time to indulge in the luxury of friendships!

We have all been created so uniquely. We all have different strengths and weaknesses, likes and dislikes. It is only when we truly come together that we can begin to enjoy the fullness of what God has created in us. The truth of the matter is that we need one another. Together we can spur and encourage one another on, as our strengths and weaknesses complement each other. We have the potential to become so much stronger as an individual *because* of our relationships with one another. In fact, it is when we are together that we form not only family, but a mighty army. This is why the punishment of solitary confinement is such an effective tool used by correctional services. People have been known to go insane over an extended period of time when the possibility of relationships has been withheld. The disciples once asked Jesus which was the greatest commandment, to which He replied:

> "*Love the Lord your God* with all your heart and with all your soul and with all your mind." This is the first and greatest commandment. And the second is like it [in other words, just as important]: "*Love your neighbour* as yourself." All the Law and the Prophets hang on these two commandments"
>
> (Matthew 22:37–40, NIV, my italics)

It is incredible to think that it is just as important to love those around us as it is to love the God who created the universe! I know of many Christians today who spend hours working on their relationship with God and who spend precious little time working on relationships with others. I specifically chose the word "working" because the reality is that in order to build meaningful relationships much work and effort are involved. It means that we need to make *time* in our busy schedules to build our relationships. To pursue someone takes *time*; it takes *time* to build trust in a relationship. It takes *time* in a relationship to develop an understanding of where others are at. How many times have I not wished for a day to be longer than twenty-four hours, just so that I could fit more in to my already hectic schedule? Time, time, time; so much needed but so little of it! I have often been aware of times when Satan has used the tactic: "If I can't slow her down, I'll push her so fast from behind that she won't know her head from her tail!"

It used to be that in these incredibly busy seasons that I tended to slip into a mindset where people became my little projects and it was only recently that I was challenged to my core on this very issue. You see, I was doing all the right things, pursuing relationships, meeting with and praying for ladies and even seeing God do amazing things in their lives as He brought them to a place of wholeness. At the start of each week, I would ponder and pray as to who God would have me meet with that week and then promptly phone or email them to arrange a time to get together. During the meeting, I would patiently listen to where they were at and possibly even give them godly advice as to what their next step in life should be. We would then pray together and soon it would be time to leave. It was at this point that I would mentally tick them off my little to-do list for the day, as I moved on to my next project.

Suddenly, I felt a spotlight shine into the depths of my

heart as I began to examine how much I really loved these women. I knew that I had cared enough to make the time to meet with them, but did I really *love* them? Jesus asked Peter this very question the first time He met with him after His resurrection: "Simon... do you *truly* love me...?" (John 21:15, NIV). When Paul wrote to the Corinthians, he could not have made it more clear then when he said, "If I... have not love, I am only a resounding gong or a clanging cymbal" (1 Corinthians 13:1, NIV). I don't know about you but I certainly want to be more than a clanging cymbal!

How do we do it, then? Do we continue to say, "As soon as such and such is over, I will begin to pursue relationships?" Are our circumstances ever going to change? Maybe – if you have very small children, then yes, that full-on, possibly difficult stage of being at home with your young ones will pass. Maybe you are in the middle of studying for an important exam; then yes, for you, your busy season too will soon come to an end. As for me, my daughters are fourteen and eleven and they are both at school from 9 a.m. until just after 3 p.m. This is the amount of time that I have at my disposal and have allocated to building relationships with those other than my family. My husband and I head up an incredibly active resource church. This means that for me right now, and for the foreseeable future, I do not think my circumstances will change much. I have therefore stopped thinking at the start of a new year that "At least it can't get any busier than last year!" The thing that I have come to realize is that it is such a joy and a privilege to serve our King and the Body of Christ, and I trust that most of the time my busyness is fruitful. There are seasons in each one of our lives when we are running at a faster pace. If these seasons of busyness are God-ordained, then He will give us the grace and the capacity to run the race without losing our peace. The writer of Proverbs warns us about the dangers of being a sluggard and it is important to continually assess our lives so that we can find a healthy balance.

It saddens me when I see how some people associate busyness with importance; when they struggle to differentiate between being busy and being productive and fruitful. There was a time in my life when busyness was part of my coping mechanism. I used to hide behind my busyness and even try and add things to my already manic schedule, rather than face up to whatever emotional situation I was facing. I am not usually into reality television, but have found myself glued to *I'm a Celebrity... Get Me Out of Here!* I have been amazed that two of the celebrities have spoken about the fact that in their boredom, they have found their whole experience in the jungle to be surprisingly emotional. It is only as they sit around their fire with nothing to do that their minds are afforded the luxury of revisiting past hurts and traumas. Although Esther Rantzen lost her husband a number of years ago, it was only in this environment that she was able to allow fresh and unexpected emotions to well up. No matter how hard we try to bury our hurts or pretend they'll just go away, there will come a time when our emotions must come to the surface.

Unfortunately, however, there are times when we get so busy, even when we are being fruitful, that some of our spinning plates actually do drop! In different seasons there are different plates, but I would imagine that it is quite common for our relationship with God to be one of the first things that is neglected when we are under too much pressure. It could also be our relationship with our husband or our children that suffers; sometimes it is the housework or that infamous pile of ironing that we fall behind with.

What about spending time enjoying the company of our friends – does that suffer when we are too busy? It is so important that we re-evaluate our priorities on a regular basis. We need to perform regular check-ups on how we are managing our time and I believe that God will give us the wisdom necessary to make appropriate adjustments in our lives.

Time with God

Joanna Weaver in *Having a Mary Heart in a Martha World* uses a very apt illustration. She quotes from J. Sidlow Baxter as he describes his battle to establish a regular devotional time. He writes:

> As never before, my will and I stood face to face. I asked my will the straight question, "Will, are you ready for an hour of prayer?" Will answered, "Here I am, and I'm quite ready, if you are." So Will and I linked arms and turned to go for our time of prayer. At once all the emotions began pulling the other way and protesting, "We're not coming." I saw Will stagger just a bit, so I asked, "Can you stick it out Will?" and Will replied, "Yes, if you can." So Will went, and we got down to prayer... It was a struggle all the way through. At one point... one of the traitorous emotions had snared my imagination and had run off to the golf course; and it was all I could do to drag the wicked rascal back...
>
> At the end of that hour, if you had asked me, "Have you had a 'good time'?" I would have had to reply, "No, it has been a wearying wrestle with contrary emotions and a truant imagination from

beginning to end." What is more, that battle with
the emotions continued for between two and three
weeks, and if you had asked me at the end of that
period, "Have you had a 'good time' in your daily
praying?" I would have had to confess, "No, at times
it has seemed as though the heavens were brass,
and God too distant to hear, and the Lord Jesus
strangely aloof, and prayer accomplishing nothing."

Yet something *was* happening. For one thing,
Will and I really taught the emotions that we
were completely independent of them. Also, one
morning, about two weeks after the contest began,
just when Will and I were going for another time of
prayer, I overheard one of the emotions whisper to
the other, "Come on, you guys, it's no use wasting
any more time resisting: they'll go just the same."...

Then, another couple of weeks later, what do
you think happened? During one of our prayer
times, when Will and I were no more thinking of the
emotions than of the man in the moon, one of the
most vigorous of the emotions unexpectedly sprang
up and shouted, "Hallelujah!" at which all the other
emotions exclaimed, "Amen!" And for the first time
the whole of my being – intellect, will, and emotions
– was united in one coordinated prayer-operation.
All at once, God was real, heaven was open, the
Lord Jesus was luminously present, and the Holy
Spirit was indeed moving through my longings,
and prayer was surprisingly vital. Moreover, in
that instant there came a sudden realization that
heaven had been watching and listening all the
way through those days of struggle against chilling

moods and mutinous emotions; also that I had
been undergoing necessary tutoring by my heavenly
Teacher.[2]

I felt comforted to know that I was not a lone ranger in
my battle! Our most important priority is, without doubt,
spending time with our Father. This is one relationship that
we need to prioritize above all others. So many Scriptures
indicate that although God earnestly longs to commune
with us, we too carry the responsibility to respond to His
desire for intimacy with us.

> "For I know the plans I have for you," declares the
> Lord, "plans to prosper you and not to harm you,
> plans to give you hope and a future. Then *you* will
> call upon me and come and pray to me, and I will
> listen to you. *You* will seek me and find me when
> you seek me with all your heart. I will be found by
> *you*," declares the Lord...
>
> *(Jeremiah 29:11–14, NIV, my italics)*

Another Scripture that reinforces this idea is:

> Here I am! I stand at the door and knock. If anyone
> hears my voice and opens the door, I will come in
> and eat with him, and he with me.
>
> *(Revelation 3:20, NIV)*

I have heard this Scripture used when preaching a message
of salvation but it was actually written to the church in
Laodicea. These people knew God but had somehow closed
the door of their hearts to Him. Jesus extends the invitation
– the invitation is *always* there. How do we respond to it?
We need to guard and even fight for our intimate times

with the Father. The enemy will do *anything* to keep us from entering that place of intimacy. This is why I believe that Satan drives us so fast from behind. Be wise with what you say "yes" to in life and be just as wise with your "no"! Let us not miss out by ignoring God's invitation:

> Arise, come, my darling; my beautiful one, come with me.
>
> (*Song of Songs 2:13b, NIV*)

I have vacillated from being almost legalistic in my quiet times to being so casual that it hardly ever happened. I am now at a place where, hopefully, I have found more balance. I usually spend time reading the Word when I get into bed at night. It is so important to not allow the reading of good Christian books to replace our time spent in the Word. I spend time praying whenever and wherever the opportunity presents itself. This could be while doing housework, or even while I am driving my car. It is wonderful that the Holy Spirit goes wherever we go and we can remain plugged into our source throughout the day.

> Remain in me, and I will remain in you. No branch can bear fruit by itself; it must remain in the vine. Neither can you bear fruit unless you remain in me. I am the vine; you are the branches. If a man remains in me and I in him, he will bear much fruit; apart from me you can do nothing. If anyone does not remain in me, he is like a branch that is thrown away and withers; such branches are picked up, thrown into the fire and burned. If you remain in me and my words remain in you, ask whatever you wish, and it will be given you.
>
> (*John 15:4–7, NIV*)

It is so clear that we are to *remain* in Him – this is continuous and not something we switch on or off. Apart from Him, we can do nothing.

However, in today's society, the importance of *self* has been emphasized to the point where many of us have lost sight of posterity (legacy and inheritance), something that was very important in my grandparents' generation. Unfortunately, the focus today, in a postmodern society, has shifted to the place where the pursuit of *personal happiness* has become all-consuming, and many people seem to live for themselves and their own immediate gratification. The Scriptures are clear concerning our priorities in life.

> But seek first his kingdom and his righteousness,
> and all these things will be given to you as well.
>
> (Matthew 6:33, NIV)

Time with My Husband

Spending quality time with Michael is another area that I have learned to fiercely guard. Since we have been in the ministry, we have always operated in the knowledge that Mondays are our day off. For many years we struggled to put this into practice and, because of our great love for the people, we often found it hard to say no if we were needed on a Monday. We have realized over the years that there are *always* going to be people with needs and many "desperate" situations can usually wait until Tuesday! We regularly do something special together on a Monday while the girls are at school, and I have come to treasure these times.

We both love to walk and often in the evenings we go for a brisk walk around the block. In the busyness of life, it is so easy to slip into a place where we are "living past each other" and, by walking together regularly, we are not only exercising, we are also enjoying the opportunity to catch up with one another.

We have trained and released incredible leaders in Jubilee Church who now take care of many of the pastoral issues with which we would have previously dealt. There are always going to be pressing needs and I have found a tendency in some people to want to "suck us dry". As we have put boundaries into our marriage, we have enjoyed a more ordered lifestyle where we are no longer at the beck and call of the multitudes.

We are focused on what God has called us to do and, at this stage of our lives, our primary relationships are with our eldership team. God has blessed us with a wonderful team of men and women who are not only sold out to the vision and purposes of God, but who would literally give their lives for one another. The unity, loyalty and deep friendships we have with each another is certainly not something we take for granted. I can honestly say that I genuinely look forward to the times when we meet together.

Michael is, by nature, fun-loving and this is one aspect of his personality that has been reproduced in the lives of our people. A leader once said to his leaders, "Never underestimate how bored your people really are!" When we are able to maintain an element of fun in our meetings, it is somehow easier to embrace busy seasons. We laugh so much in Jubilee and have first-hand knowledge of the fact that "the joy of the Lord is [our] strength" (Nehemiah 8:10, NIV).

Time with My Children

Some time ago, I read a book by Elizabeth George entitled *A Woman after God's own Heart*. After reading it, I felt compelled to guard my time with my girls. As a result, I no longer meet with people once Amy and Sarah get home from school. This means that I am there to talk to them about their day, to help them, or supervise any homework that needs doing, and to prepare the evening meal. There are times when they are actively involved in helping me in the kitchen and there are times when they just potter around. In fact, most of the time, Amy is invariably singing at the top of her voice, while Sarah is usually either twirling around the kitchen or perfecting the cartwheel. Whatever they are doing, I think it is vitally important for their security, knowing that I am available should they need me. I know that they love spending quality time with both Michael and I because I see how their faces light up at the mere thought of doing something special together.

These are precious times and I guard them with my life. I know that in the not too distant future there will be a time when the girls will leave home to start their own lives, so I need to make the most of the time I have with them now. I know that many mothers, especially mums who need to work a full day, find this subject brings feelings of overwhelming guilt. Be aware that the enemy will jump on the bandwagon and actually plot and scheme for us to remain in a place of bondage because of our guilt. Jesus came to earth to set the captives free, so be free! He knows your heart and covers our inadequacies and shortcomings.

Time for Myself

Another priority I have made is "me" time. I know this probably sounds selfish but I have realized that without investing time into my own well-being I have nothing of worth to give. Three times a week (usually without fail) my first thirty minutes after getting the girls off to school are spent at the gym. I love this time on my own. I can switch off completely as I move from one exercise machine to the next. There are so many benefits to be gained from regular exercise but, for me, the most important one is that I de-stress. I can literally feel any tension work its way out of my system. I also sleep much better when I have exercised. I can honestly say that if I waited for the right opportunity to present itself for me to go, I would never get there!

I also love to bake and as the girls are getting older, they love to come alongside me in the kitchen, usually with the motivation of licking out the bowl! I find baking to be both rewarding and therapeutic. Again, it is a time where I can either be praying or switch off completely (unless the girls are with me).

Another area I see as an investment of my time is reading. I remember as a young girl literally ploughing through book after book, often until the early hours of the morning. It came as a surprise when I realized that I had not picked up a book for ages, when the girls were very young. It was only when we started the mentoring programme that I was able to get back to regular reading. Now there is always a book next to my bed, sometimes even two or three at a time. I also see this as "me" time, not only a time where I can unwind and relax but also a time of receiving as I glean from the great men and women who have gone before us. Reading is such an important discipline in our lives; I cannot emphasize enough the importance of regular reading.

Time to Dream

I realize that God has placed so much within us that can only be properly tapped into if time allows.Creativity needs time to be fed in order for it to grow and develop. Do we allow ourselves time to dream in God? Are there dreams that we carry in our hearts that are so deeply buried in our busyness that they are never given room to come to the surface? It is important that we set aside time purely for the purpose of dreaming with God for greater things. This does not need to happen on a regular basis but it needs to happen consistently in order to stay in step with His Spirit.

Hazel and I both spent many years dreaming of writing a book and in the busyness of life, this particular dream could easily have been swallowed up and forgotten. We have had to fight hard to get this book written. We have had to set aside time and lay things down in order for this dream to become a reality.

I also remember a time when Michael and I were dreaming about establishing a resource hub in Maidstone. Where this was once merely a dream, it has now become a reality – not through the flick of a switch but rather through knowing the call of God for our lives and then working incredibly hard to see it come to fruition.

Time for Others

I remember when Michael and I were first married. As far as I was concerned, he was the only one I needed in life. I remember saying to him that I would be quite happy with just the two of us living on a desert island. You can imagine how horrified I was when I realized that he did not feel quite the same way! It was not a question of whether or not he loved me but he realized how important friendships are in our lives. For the first six months of our marriage, I had seriously neglected spending time with my girlfriends and Michael was the one who encouraged me to continue to pursue these relationships.

We have already looked at the whole subject of friendships but I would like to emphasize here the importance of building godly relationships on various different levels. Firstly, it is vital that we make time for those whom we have asked to speak into our lives. It is a dangerous assumption to make that we can speak freely into the lives of others without first ensuring that we too are walking in an accountable relationship. We need to seek out these people and set aside specific time to nurture these relationships. If you have not yet identified someone who is able to speak into your life on a very intimate level, then ask God to show you who this should be. It needs to be someone who is spiritually more mature than you are, someone walking in godly wisdom. We all need someone that we can trust to help us implement godly boundaries.

Another type of relationship that we need to make time for is with those who we consider to be our peers. An example of this is David's relationship with Jonathan. It is in the context of this type of relationship that we can share our hearts and have fun together. It is also here that we encourage and spur one another on as we progress on our journey of life. We need to be putting aside time to allow these relationships to blossom, as the gift of friendship given by God is one to be cherished.

The example of Paul's relationship with Timothy highlights a third area in which we need to invest our time and energy. It is in these relationships that we enjoy the privilege of speaking into the lives of others. In Paul's letter to Titus, he urges the older women to train the younger women. "But I am not old!" you may be saying. The truth is there is *always* someone younger than you. It is the responsibility of each generation to impart and reproduce that which God has entrusted to them to the next generation.

We have an obligation to make time for others and we need to pursue relationships in all these areas. This is what God intended for us and I know that my life has been incredibly enriched because of the women that God has placed in my life.

Although in theory I'll always endeavour to put my family first, before ministry, there are times where God has required more of me. I often think back to a particularly busy season in our lives while we were living in Queenstown, South Africa. As a church, we had recently purchased a farm which needed to be transformed into a training centre. This included renovating a six-bedroom house, converting a triple garage into a lecture hall, and fixing the swimming pool! The task seemed overwhelming as we did not have the finances to enable us to call on the services of a building company. It was down to those who were willing and available, with experience and expertise not being a prerequisite.

Our daughter Amy was a toddler at the time. Anyone who has been through this stage will know that a building site is not the best or safest place for a toddler! This resulted in me often being stuck at home with Amy while Michael spent many long days and nights working extremely hard with our team of volunteer helpers, preparing our new facility. Everyone was buzzing with excitement – everyone except me! I felt deprived, not only of not being part of things, but also because of the fact that for nearly three months we had not been able to enjoy any quality time together as a family. I was beginning to resent this.

One Sunday after church, as I was driving home with Amy, I cried out to God in frustration: "God, what are we doing here? It is not good for our family to spend so much time apart!"

His reply was almost audible as He gently threw the question straight back at me: "So what are you doing here?" A bit annoyed – I was the one meant to be asking the questions! – I replied that we were establishing His kingdom in Queenstown. He then asked me what His word said about "kingdom". Now, I have to say that at that point in time, the only Scripture I could think of that referred to God's kingdom was the well-known verses in Matthew that read, "But seek first his kingdom and his righteousness, and all these things will be given to you as well" (Matthew 6:33, NIV).

He needed to say no more. I knew that my selfish attitude had been wrong and, for that particular season, establishing the training centre needed to be a priority. There were deadlines to meet and new students waiting to move in. When Michael got home late that night, I asked him for his forgiveness and told him that I was now at a place where I could release him to get on with the job that he was doing. I cannot even begin to describe how much pressure seemed to literally melt off the situation. I had come to a place of peace and was thus able to begin to draw on an incredible outpouring of God's grace to walk the rest of that road. Recently, I read *Making Jesus Lord* in which Loren Cunningham explores the dynamic power of laying down our rights. For that season, I needed to lay down my right to family time, knowing that because of

God's faithfulness, what He gives in return is of far greater value.

> Come to me, *all* you who are weary and burdened,
> and I will give you rest. Take my yoke upon you and
> learn from me, for I am gentle and humble in heart,
> and you will find rest for your souls. For my yoke is
> easy and my burden is light.
>
> (Matthew 11:28–30, NIV, *my italics*)

The reality is that life is not actually going to slow down. There is one last area that I would like to cover before we conclude this chapter and it comes with the question: "Where is it that you run to when the ache in your heart becomes unbearable?" I know that there are many different answers to this question. Some of us find comfort in eating, while others may lose themselves in the lives of soap opera characters. Some go into a place of denial and feel that by pretending that the problem is not there, it will somehow automatically disappear. If only! For me, I seem to get busier. It was a sobering reality when I realized that instead of running into the arms of Jesus, the One who is able to comfort me in my times of pain and suffering, I would get out the vacuum cleaner and clean the house. Ridiculous, isn't it?

There is a safe place we can run to; we do not have to hide. We need to guard our hearts and ensure we face the challenges that come our way, instead of hiding behind our busy schedules. When the pressure is on, let us not get swallowed up in busyness. Rather, let us be empowered as we spend time in His presence and pursue the most important relationships in our lives.

NOTES

1 Joanna Weaver, *Having a Mary Heart in a Martha World*, Colorado Springs, Colorado: WaterBrook Press, 2000.

2 Joanna Weaver, *Having a Mary Heart in a Martha World*, Colorado Springs, Colorado: WaterBrook Press, 2000.

7

A Bun in the Oven

Reproducing Ourselves in Others

by Heather and Hazel

When God saved you He had much more than you
on His mind.

Michael Puffett

Heather writes...

We realized the work God was doing in our lives
was not just about our personal restoration
and freedom. When God saved us, He had more
than us on His mind. He was thinking about the nations!
Have you ever thought of it like that? As Hazel and l looked
around, we saw countless other women who seemed as
trapped and helpless as we had been and we decided it was
time for action; time to start investing our time and energy
into the lives of those around us. Some were desperate
for change, while others had not even realized that there
could be more. Almost all, however, longed for deeper, more
meaningful friendships in their lives. For the first time,

Hazel and I felt confident in the fact that we had something to contribute; we had been blessed in order that we could be a blessing.

Our lives, like a lump of dough, had been transformed by the yeast of the Holy Spirit.

Did you know, according to biologists, that yeast is a plant capable of reproducing itself? Without yeast, our lives remain flat and hard but as we allow the Holy Spirit to work within us, we are able to rise up. We had experienced first-hand God's healing power in our lives and we knew we carried a message of freedom for others. It was time to pioneer, launch and lead a mentoring programme, firstly within Jubilee and, later, further afield.

"Mentoring" is a commonly used word in all walks of life. We hear about it in schools, in the workplace, and in more and more churches. So what, then, does it mean to mentor someone? Within the church context, I believe mentoring is a relational experience where we walk alongside the ladies that God has entrusted to us for a given season, building a strong relationship founded on trust, honesty and accountability. Jesus set us such an awesome example in the way He faithfully built relationships with His twelve, and consequently:

> When they saw the courage of Peter and John and realized that they were *unschooled, ordinary* men, they were astonished and they took note that these men *had been with Jesus*.
>
> (Acts 4:13, NIV, my italics)

His mere presence with these men had rubbed off on them to the extent that others took notice. Mentoring is not about imparting head knowledge. We could go to Bible school if we wanted more head knowledge! No, mentoring is about helping others find God. We would be horrified if the ladies we mentored ever looked to us for all the answers.

The freedom that we have to speak into their lives comes from them having a clear knowledge that our hearts are *for* them and that we care about them as individuals. Our relationships are therefore purposeful. The strategy and goal-setting that does occur is birthed out of a solid relationship and not the other way around.

Sharing God-given resources is also very much at the heart of what we seek to do. We never want others to become dependent upon us but rather to gain a firm understanding of all that God can give them as they seek to grow in their relationship with Him. We have been so blessed in all that God has poured into our lives and our desire is to impart these truths into the lives of others. There are also numerous books and resources we can recommend that have been life-changing (these are listed at the end of this book).

The following points give a brief summary of what mentoring is and what it is not:

1. We encourage the ladies to view mentoring as a *lifestyle* rather than "just another meeting". It should not be seen as a time where women get together for either a bit of gossip or a chance to lick and compare wounds over a cup of tea.

2. Mentoring is a *safe place* where confidentiality is foremost in our minds, creating an environment where we are able to be completely real with one another. We understand the principles of submission and authority, and find safety and security in remaining in that place.

It is definitely not birthed in rebellion with the thinking: "Anything the men can do, we can do better!"

3. Committing to a year of mentoring is a season of *spiritual growth* that is fostered through regular studying of the Word; meeting and praying with a prayer partner on a weekly basis and a generally more disciplined lifestyle. Mentoring should not be seen as a mental or academic exercise with an opportunity to merely grow in head knowledge.

Hazel writes...

Imitate me, just as I also imitate Christ.

(1 Corinthians 11:1, NKJV)

Herein lies the heart of mentoring. Paul's bold statement in 1 Corinthians 11:1, "Imitate me," is instantly qualified by the condition, "… just as I also imitate Christ." Because of his relationship with the Corinthian church, Paul desired to share his God-given resources and longed that they would learn to imitate the *Christ* in him. How well we know Him will determine how effectively we imitate Him. Of course, there is always further to go in this process. We each, therefore, have a responsibility to be constantly pressing into Him and spending time investing in our relationship with Him, just as He so faithfully invests in us. In essence, when I stop "imitating Christ", there is nothing of significance in me worth imitating.

When Heather and I first launched the ladies' mentoring programme in Jubilee, we wrestled long and hard with the question, "What qualifies us to lead?" and soon realized that it has to start somewhere, with someone who is willing to be that *first generation*. We were both aware that this was something He had entrusted to us and that He would therefore empower us to carry it out, but we had to fight off the feelings of inadequacy.

So, together – and with much apprehension – we stepped out... and we have not looked back since! God is so incredibly faithful. He desires not only to meet with us but to dwell amongst us and bring us to a place of wholeness. So often He moves not because of us but despite us, and in those times when we have felt at our weakest, He has broken in and manifested His presence.

Reproducing ourselves is a key biblical principle that we see flowing throughout creation itself.

> Then God said, "Let the earth bring forth the living creature according to its *kind*..."
>
> (Genesis 1:24, NKJV)

We were designed by the great Creator Himself to reproduce after our own kind. For example, when I gave birth, I had human babies rather than baby elephants! We have been made in the image of God, and therefore we carry within us attributes of our Maker.

When Jesus walked the earth, He reflected and represented His Father.

In Genesis 1:16, we read about two lights – the greater light (the sun) and the lesser light (the moon). The moon has no light of its own but rather reflects its light from the sun. Jesus did this with the Father, radiating and reflecting His Father in all that He said and did, always giving God the glory. Jesus was an ambassador on behalf of the Father, accurately representing and reflecting Him. In the same way, we carry no light of our own, but as His children we reflect His light in our lives. As His ambassadors, we have a responsibility to accurately represent Jesus Christ in the way that we conduct our lives; as we represent and reflect Jesus through our lives, it is inevitable that we will reproduce this in others, so that together we become children of the light, always directing and reflecting the focus back to Jesus.

Heather writes...

I believe that God works in us for reasons beyond ourselves and our needs. Take a moment to consider the Dead Sea. The Dead Sea is 30 per cent saltier than the ocean which means that no macroscopic aquatic organisms such as fish or water plants can live in it. Although there is plenty of water flowing into the Dead Sea, there is nothing flowing out of it, resulting in a stagnant body of water that is unable to sustain life. Similarly, in our lives, unless there is an outworking of the goodness of God, we run the risk of becoming stagnant; inward-looking and self-centred.

As we began to comprehend the fact that God could actually use us, He began to birth within us the desire to walk beside other women in a more structured and purposeful way. When we launched the mentoring programme in Jubilee, we had absolutely no systems or any administration in place – we simply worked it out as we went along. God works despite us, certainly not because of us, and when we make ourselves available He is ready and waiting to work with us and through us. What a privilege!

We started small, and in our first year invited our key leaders on board, trusting that they would then go on to lead groups the following year. It felt quite risky with none of us having ever walked a mentoring road with anyone before, but we were acutely aware of Him leading and guiding us. With each new year of mentoring, we have grown a little more in our understanding of how best to administrate, facilitate and lead. Some ladies choose to sign up again and again, while others see it as a one-off. The thing I love about mentoring is that each year feels like a new adventure.

During our first year of mentoring, the focus was very much on building deeper and more meaningful relationships amongst the ladies, as there was a strong desire for solid friendships. I remember how we put two of the most unlikely ladies together as prayer partners; Justine, at that stage, young and single, and Susie who was in her late thirties with a husband and two children. Today they still chuckle as they think back on the first time they met together, both baffled by what they could possibly have in common. The amazing thing was that an incredible friendship was birthed between these two women as they met regularly to pray. This friendship has seen them through many different seasons in their lives – particularly Justine, who is now married and in leadership in Jubilee Church.

Our second year was one in which God seemed to be dealing mostly with incorrect mindsets and we had the privilege of walking with the ladies to a greater measure of freedom as they embraced the truth of God's Word in their lives. Joyce Meyer's book, *Battlefield of the Mind* was used as a tool to bring a deeper understanding of the fact that:

> ... our struggle is not against flesh and blood, but against the rulers, against the authorities, against the powers of this dark world and against the spiritual forces of evil in the heavenly realms.
>
> (Ephesians 6:12, NIV)

During our third year, the emphasis was on the question, "Into whose life are you reproducing what God has given you?" Again, this goes back to the understanding of the fact that God had more than us on His mind when He saved us. This truth allowed the ladies to become far more mindful of those around them, realizing that where they had learned to overcome could be modelled to the next generation.

The focus during our fourth year of mentoring was to develop and grow in our understanding of God's kingdom and who we are as daughters of the King. As we looked at the various stages of maturity in the life of a Christian, we began to identify with the ladies, and understand where they were at. I remember one particular lady who really desired to be a mentoring leader. As she walked out the mentoring journey she began to recognize that, despite being saved for a number of years, she was still very much in the toddler stage of development. This understanding brought about a real sense of security as she released herself from the pressure of having to be someone she was not yet ready to be.

At the time of writing, we are in our fifth year of mentoring and so far we have spent a lot of time meditating and reading about the empowering grace of God. We can all testify to stories of the outworking of grace in our lives and, as we learn to shift our focus onto Jesus and live with an attitude of gratitude, we can begin to appropriate His grace, empowered to walk the road He has called us to.

Paul's exhortation to Titus encapsulates the heart of reproducing what God has done in our lives in the lives of others:

> Older women likewise are to be reverent in their
> behaviour, not malicious gossips nor enslaved to

much wine, teaching what is good, so that they may
encourage the young women to love their husbands,
to love their children, to be sensible, pure, workers
at home, kind, being subject to their own husbands,
so that the word of God will not be dishonoured.

(Titus 2:3–5, NASB)

Although we are not sure what the future holds, one thing
we know for sure is that He has been incredibly faithful in
leading and guiding us on our journey so far. We know that
we can find comfort and rest in the knowledge that He will
continue to show us the way forward as long as we remain
available.

8

Top Down, Inside Out
Reasoning from the Whole to the Part

by Heather

If you don't know where you are going, any road will get you there.

Lewis Carroll

There have been occasions in my life when I have struggled to make sense of it all, when I could only see very small bits of a much bigger picture and have ended up feeling confused. I have often used the illustration of the embroidered quilt – the "blanket" between us and God. God has the best seat in the house because He gets to see the quilt of our lives the right way up. He can see the whole picture and can make sense of what is going on, where it is all going and where it will end up! We, on the other hand, can only see it from underneath, with a not-so-clear perspective. All we get to see are the dangling threads as chapters of our lives have opened and closed in different colours.

The thing that I have learned through this is that it is so

129

important to always reason from the *whole* to the *part*. In other words, see the bigger picture first and then break it down into bite-sized chunks. This thinking has often helped me to keep a clear perspective on things and sometimes even enabled me to make some sense of my life.

For me, the bigger picture is God and His kingdom. Jesus came to bring us a message of good news, a message of hope and freedom and the opportunity to live life to the full. He had only three years with the twelve men into whom He poured His life and I am convinced that He would not have wasted precious time by teaching them – and the crowds that followed Him – about trivial issues. In fact, in Luke 4:43, Jesus said, "I must preach the good news of the *kingdom of God* to the other towns also, because *that is why I was sent*" (NIV, my italics). After His resurrection and before His ascension into heaven, His time was even more limited and He used that time to teach that which was most important. In Acts 1:3b we read that "He appeared to them over a period of forty days and spoke about the *kingdom of God*" (NIV, my italics).

So how did Jesus actually go about teaching His unlearned friends? Being a primary school teacher myself, I understand the importance of using language that those who are being taught can relate to. Children are able to understand a new concept much faster if they are able to compare it with something with which they are already familiar. This is why, over and over again, Jesus said, "The kingdom of heaven is like..." or "The kingdom of God is like..." By looking at only a few chapters in the book of Matthew we read, for example, that He compared the kingdom of God to a farmer sowing seeds on different types of soil (Matthew 13:1–23), to a mustard seed (Matthew 13:31), to a treasure hidden in a field (Matthew 13:44), to a merchant looking for fine pearls (Matthew 13:45), to a net used in fishing (Matthew 13:47), to a king who wanted to settle accounts with his servants (Matthew 18:23), and even to a landowner who hired men to work in his vineyard (Matthew 20:1). The list goes on and on!

I have learned many valuable lessons in my Christian walk but one of the most life-changing revelations I have had is in my understanding of God's kingdom and who we are as His children. *Who I am* and *what I do* in life is now rooted in my love for my Father, rather than trying to earn His favour. I have come to understand that we are human *be*ings, not human *do*ings. I know many people who run about quite frantically as they try to earn God's love, but it is *who we are* that pleases God immensely; there is nothing that I can do that will influence the unconditional love that He has towards me. When God introduced Jesus as His Son, He said, "This is My beloved Son, in whom I am well pleased" (Matthew 3:17), NKJV. It is important to note that Jesus had not yet done a single thing; He was not even in full-time ministry and yet God was pleased with Him. It is only when I reach a place where I am secure in who I am in Him that I am motivated to do the good works that have been prepared in advance for me – from a place of *being* rather than *doing* (Ephesians 2:10).

The word "kingdom" is made up of two words: 'king', meaning the ruler and 'dom', meaning the domain of the king. In other words, a kingdom is the area in which a king rules and reigns. The Greek word for "kingdom" is *basileia*, which means "the influence, rule and reign of the king". In a biblical context, it means "God's government, rulership and dominion". God's kingdom is not a *physical* kingdom:

> My kingdom is not of this world. If it were, my
> servants would fight to prevent my arrest by the
> Jews. But now my kingdom is from another place.
>
> (John 18:36, NIV)

Rather, God's kingdom is a *spiritual* kingdom, one that is
established in the hearts of men and women:

> The kingdom of God does not come with your
> careful observation, nor will people say, 'Here it is,'
> or 'There it is,' *because the kingdom of God is within
> you.*
>
> (Luke 17:21, NIV)

As a church, we have been looking for opportunities to bless
our local community. Over the years, we have developed
good relationships with some of the key, influential people
who also serve in our local area. One committee organizes
a huge annual summer fair, the proceeds of which go to
charity. I know that these people, most of whom are elderly
now, really appreciate our help and involvement in the fair
every year and are amazed by the degree of wholeness that
they have seen in the young adults from Jubilee Church.
One lady from this committee also founded a pre-school
based in a community hall near our training centre. When
we noticed that this community hall was looking a little
worse for wear, we volunteered to redecorate the whole
facility for them, radically cutting down on their expenses.

Although I am not sure if they understand the whole
idea of us wanting to be a blessing, expecting nothing in
return, I know that they really do love and trust us. More
and more they are approaching us for help and advice
and one man even made a comment about how he had

underestimated the relevance of the church today. Slowly but surely, as we demonstrate kingdom and godly principles to our community, I believe that the love of Christ becomes tangible on a personal level.

Because God's kingdom is a spiritual kingdom, established within our hearts, we are able to carry within us the "rule and reign of God". I believe that we have grossly underestimated the degree to which this knowledge can change our spheres of influence in our communities and workplaces.

How did Jesus do it? Much to the dismay of the Pharisees – and even some of His well-meaning disciples – Jesus constantly broke tradition as He fellowshipped over meals with both Gentiles and sinners. As He spent time with these unlikely people, He established *His influence*, thus bringing about a transformation in their lives.

We often refer to God's kingdom as being a *top down, inside out* kingdom. Because God is the King of His kingdom, we operate within the mindset of His kingdom being a theocracy. (This is very different to a democracy where everyone has a say in what happens!) As the King of His kingdom, God imparts His heart to human beings (top down) and thus brings about an *internal transformation*, which in turn leads to *external impact* (inside out). As we grow and mature in our relationship with God, we grow in *internal government*. This means that we know and understand that there is a time and place for everything; that there is a godly order in our lives because of God's authority within us. As leaders, we are aware of the need to take up our responsibility and govern God's people in a way that is in line with kingdom principles. Moses is a really good example of a man who led and governed God's people according to the commands of God, even though he made many mistakes along the way! He was certainly not a leader who felt the need to win any popularity contests amongst more than a million Israelites who felt they would have been better off staying as slaves in Egypt.

The way that we have set up our mentoring programme within Jubilee Church allows us to speak into the lives of the ladies who have submitted themselves to the leadership of Jubilee. These ladies are at a place where they are hungry for spiritual growth. We believe this can be achieved through relationship and accountability, as well as a balance between love and godly leadership.

As I listened to a group of ladies sharing their testimonies at our recent end of year mentoring banquet, I was able to identify a single thread that had been woven through all of their lives; they had all grown so much in the area of self-discipline. In other words, they have begun to see the kingdom of God come in their own hearts and lives. Without internal government, we become like little boats tossed about in the waves in whichever direction the wind takes us.

Let's face it, no matter how much the spirit is willing, the flesh is weak (Matthew 26:41). Wouldn't we all be so mature if we were able to grow merely through our good intentions? I am sure that each one of us could improve on the amount of time we spend praying and reading the Word of God, so why then is this still a problem in the church today? I believe that the answer lies with our level of internal government. I love Richard Foster's *Celebration of Discipline*, in which he examines the importance of several disciplines that are fundamental to furthering our growth as Christians. Emphasizing the basics, he reiterates significant disciplines such as reading the Word on a daily basis, regular prayer and the importance of times of solitude in our lives. John Ortberg's book, *The Life You've Always Wanted*, is another excellent and really refreshing book on spiritual disciplines in our lives.

We are not merely trying to give the ladies scaffolding to hold them up in the weak areas of their lives. Scaffolding is a temporary structure that is only able to perform and function on an external level. Our aim is to empower the ladies to lay hold of these truths for themselves, avoiding the pitfall of externally motivated dependence on us as their mentors.

I believe that a key for building God's kingdom is understanding the principle of what it means when Jesus said that we are to make disciples of all nations.

> Then Jesus came to them and said, "All authority in heaven and on earth has been given to me. Therefore go and make disciples of all nations, baptizing them in the name of the Father and of the Son and of the Holy Spirit, and teaching them to obey everything I have commanded you. And surely I am with you always, to the very end of the age."
>
> (Matthew 28:18–20, NIV)

As church today, do we even have an idea of what a "discipled nation" looks like? The Greek word for "nations" is *ethnos*, which means a tribe, nation or people group; wherever people gather together for a common purpose. In other words, *ethnos* does not only mean cultural groupings of people, it also refers to our local area where people gather together for a common purpose. Therefore schools, universities and various workplaces are also *ethnos* – or "nations". This makes the whole idea of reaching a city so much more attainable. I believe that each one of us, having grown up as mature sons and daughters with internal government, has the potential to reach and bring kingdom influence as we live our lives according to kingdom principles, to our own spheres of influence. Teachers reach out to and bring kingdom influence to other teachers, and police officers reach out to and bring kingdom influence to other police officers. This applies to all walks of life.

So, where could Hazel and I bring influence? Do you remember in chapter 1 where Hazel wrote about inviting Edna Els from South Africa to the UK to train and equip us in the whole area of mentoring? Well, we decided to invite other leaders from different churches in Maidstone to our training day and a number of churches have since started their own mentoring programmes. I realized that we were all walking a very new road and that perhaps it would be good to meet together as leaders to encourage and support one another on our new ventures. We decided to launch what we now call 'Kingdom Mentoring' and see this as an opportunity to build unity between like-minded churches.

As a group, we have been meeting on the first Monday of every month and the relationships and the unity that has developed amongst us has been an incredible blessing. At the time of writing, we are enjoying a new season in the Kingdom Mentoring as each of the church leaders has invited the next generation on board. We launched this broader vision by going away for a weekend with a heart to not only build relationships with one another but to also grow in our understanding of what it means for God's kingdom to be established here in Maidstone. I believe it is imperative that our "unity" is birthed through sound relationships, rather than being based solely on a programme to reach our city. It has surprised us to see how many initiatives in towns and cities across the UK reason from "event" to "relationship". In other words, because we have very little relationship on a daily basis, we try every year to organize a big event or evangelistic outreach which we hope will build and cement relationships. This generally does not work. We need to pursue relationship with like-minded churches *first* and then use that unity to impact our area. This is a very important distinction for us as a church.

To sum up: In God's kingdom, Father God is also our King – He is the one who rules and reigns in His kingdom. Our role in this kingdom is not one of slavery. This is the exciting part; we are daughters of the King! This means that we are the ones eligible for the inheritance. When we enter the kingdom of God, we enter into a place of order; a place of safety and security; a place where there are godly boundaries in our lives. Best of all, we enter a place where we can be with our King! Let us pray with understanding, as Jesus taught the disciples to pray, "Thy Kingdom come, Thy will be done in earth, as it is in heaven" (Matthew 6:10, KJV).

9

Who, Me? Yes, You!

Qualities of a Mentor

by Hazel

A single candle can light a thousand more without diminishing itself.

Hillel

As a small child, I remember my father taking me to the theatre to see the play *Cinderella*. What made this evening even more memorable was that I went alone with my dad and not with my sister or brother. We had booked tickets as a family but I had been ill and unable to go at the last minute. Just as I was beginning to come to terms with my disappointment, the news came that we had managed to get two tickets for a matinee performance and I would, indeed, see Cinders go to the ball after all. This was the beginning of a magical afternoon and, having been enthralled by the presence of a pony on the stage to pull Cinderella's carriage, I did not think things could reach any dizzier heights. At the end of the show, there was an invitation for children to come onto the stage and get a prize. My hand shot up and before I knew it, I was standing there beside the pantomime cast, surrounded by lights and being sung to by the man who played the character of Buttons. "Who, me?" my heart cried. "Yes, you!" came the reply. All the other children went back to their seats and I was chosen to remain and receive a lollipop... in fact, not just one lollipop, but too many to carry! Every time I went to walk off he would call me back and give me another lolly. He also gave me a record called "Tonight's the Night" (it was in the olden days of vinyl) and I must have played that record a hundred times over. To be picked out from a crowd and showered with gifts is the most amazing experience.

The title of this chapter is, 'Who, me? Yes, You!' God reaches out and speaks words of love, words of life, to each one of us. He acknowledges us. He has a plan for our lives and in response to our, "Who, me?" He cries, "Yes, you."

As the mentoring programme has evolved in Jubilee, Heather and I have identified certain qualities that we look for when asking someone to lead a mentoring group. These are not heavy, unattainable conditions but merely evidence that the prospective mentoring leader is moving forward in her journey with the Lord and embracing the road ahead.

1. A Woman of the Word

Imagine an obstacle course. Various props are set up that have to be climbed over, or crawled under, or walked along. There is a time pressure and others are watching you. You look ahead and try to anticipate what you see and how you intend to overcome each obstacle. There can be no short cuts and you will be disqualified if you fail to complete each task. Looking around, you are able to clearly distinguish the beginning from the end and the easy tasks from the more difficult ones. Having taken in your surroundings you feel confident and are ready for the challenge. You are in the starting position and eagerly leaning forward to begin your race when suddenly, from the sidelines, someone comes up and informs you that you must complete the race blindfolded. It's ridiculous. What chance do you have if you cannot see where you are going?

> Your word is a lamp to my feet
> And a light to my path.
>
> (Psalm 119:105, NKJV)

I remember Neil teaching on this verse a few years ago. To illustrate his point, he set up an obstacle course in the church auditorium and asked one of the guys to do the course. The guy did well and we all applauded but then Neil asked him to do the course again, blindfolded. You can imagine the chaos; it was impossible. Neil made the point that without the Word to illuminate our path, we are running blind.

There are many obstacles that we face in our Christian walk but His Word can bring clarity and direction like nothing else.

To imitate Christ we must know Him intimately and one of the ways that He reveals Himself to us is through His Word. His Word must be our closest friend, the light that guides our every step (Psalm 119:105), and our weapon of mass destruction. Through reading His Word, our hearts are prepared to receive His truth and our spirits are nourished, fed and enlightened.

> For the word of God is living and powerful, and
> sharper than any two-edged sword, piercing even
> to the division of soul and spirit, and of joints and

marrow, and is a discerner of the thoughts and
intents of the heart.

(Hebrews 4:12, NKJV)

As we read His Word, the thoughts and intentions of our
hearts are revealed. This is a vital process that we need
to apply to our lives, because by nature our hearts are
"deceitful above all things" (Jeremiah 17:9, NKJV).

As much as we encourage our leaders to share from
their personal experiences, what the Word of God has to say
about any given situation is of far greater relevance. What
we long to reproduce in others is not our own personal life
experiences but rather what God has revealed to us through
those experiences. We want to impart godly principles;
these are revealed through His Word and by His Spirit.

Let the word of Christ dwell in you richly in all
wisdom, teaching and admonishing one another...

(Colossians 3:16, NKJV)

The word "dwell" here means "to take up residence or
to make one's home among". The Word of God needs to
be stored up in our hearts and this only comes through
diligently reading it in and out of season.

I can recall times when I have not been able to put the
Bible down. I have stayed up late into the night, blissfully
unaware of time, lost in the pages and soaking in the truth
that is feeding me. But I also recall times when wading
through it has felt like chewing sawdust and I have found
no life in what I have read.

This is why it is essential that in the "good" seasons,
when it is easy to enter in to His presence, touch the throne
room and read His Word, we store His truth in our hearts.

What truths are in the storehouse of your heart? What do you have to draw from in the tough times? There is a great motto used by the US Marines: "The more you sweat in peace time, the less you will bleed in war."

In the times when all is calm, instead of just kicking back and giving in to passivity, we need to be preparing and training our souls for what lies ahead. Otherwise, when the onslaught comes (and I promise you it will), spiritually speaking, blood will be shed, lives will be lost and we will have to give an account for our laziness in the season of abundance.

> Your word I have hidden in my heart,
> That I might not sin against You...
> I will not forget Your word.
>
> (Psalm 119:11, 16, NKJV)

His Word enables us to walk in obedience. It protects us and helps to prevent us from walking in sin. The more heart knowledge we gain from His Word, the clearer the picture becomes of how we should live.

His Word needs to be the first place we run to in times of difficulty. Go there before you speak to your spouse, phone a friend, or even ask the audience! Although they can, at times, give good and sound advice, it is far more beneficial to firstly enquire of Him and His Word. David enquired of the Lord and he was called "a man after God's own heart". God wants us to learn to look to Him for all we need. This also protects us from having wrong expectations of others and ensures that He is our source. What does His Word say about the situation you are facing? See the Word as your companion, your friend.

His Word is also our weapon of mass destruction. How

can we fight any battle without the correct weapons? As Paul reminds us, we are not fighting flesh and blood.

> For we do not wrestle against flesh and blood, but against principalities, against powers, against the rulers of the darkness of this age, against spiritual hosts of wickedness in the heavenly places.
>
> *(Ephesians 6:12, NKJV)*

How often do we focus on the individual and allow them to become our *enemy*, when in reality we are fighting another force altogether? A good example of this is in our marriages. Satan hates marriage, especially Christian marriages built on godly principles. So often we can find ourselves fighting over silly and petty things but, when we take a step back, we see with clarity the spiritual dynamic at work.

Neil and I went through a patch where we seemed to be fighting and bickering all the time. It felt as if a wall was building between us; where we would normally communicate well with one another, we just kept missing each other. We could not seem to connect. Inside, I could feel the panic rise and I tried to analyze where we had gone wrong. It felt like a massive void had developed between us in such a small space of time, and I could hear the voice of the enemy bringing all sorts of false accusations against us. As we took a step back from attacking one another and sought God, we both realized that we were under a spiritual attack. There was no substance to our fighting and arguing. It was a smokescreen and as soon as we recognized it for what it was and resisted the enemy, the confusion lifted and our unity was restored. We need to remember that our battle is not against flesh and blood and be quick to recognize this before harm is done, harsh words are spoken and hearts are wounded. This is true of all our relationships, of course, not just marriage.

Jesus, when He was led into the wilderness, used the truth of the Scriptures as a weapon against the attacks of Satan. How can we fight effectively if we do not know the truth of His Word? In our Christian lives, and particularly when leading others, we must have a sound grasp and understanding of the Word of God.

2. A Woman Leaning Forward in the Spirit

And Jesus increased in wisdom and stature, and in favour with God and men.

(Luke 2:52, NKJV)

I love this Scripture. Here we see Jesus the boy, the Son, not yet ready to embark on the ministry prepared for Him. We can see the process, the preparation that needed to take place before He was ready to begin to fulfil His destiny. Jesus grew, or increased in wisdom and stature. It says that He also increased in favour with both God and men. Favour comes through good past reputation and causes others to open their hearts to us. Jesus was busy proving Himself in the small things. It is interesting to note that although He is the Son of God, Jesus came and endured a process through which wisdom could be gained. For us, too, there are no short cuts in the area of wisdom. Life and life's experiences are great teachers. Wisdom is soundness of judgment and a gaining of knowledge and it is not attained without a purposeful seeking and searching.

One of the qualities we look for when we consider who may be suitable to lead a mentoring group is a *leaning forward in the Spirit*. By this we mean someone who is growing in wisdom and stature; someone who is increasing in favour with both God and people. There has to be a hunger for the things of God and a straining forward in the Spirit to take a hold of all that God has to offer. We need to display qualities in our own lives that we can model to others and say, "Imitate this Christ-like quality in me... as I also imitate Christ."

3. A Woman Who will Reproduce Good Fruit

"We teach what we know, but we reproduce who we are." This is a very sobering statement and one that can often stop us from stepping out and making ourselves available. None of us are perfect and even Paul's bold statement "Imitate me" came from a heart that was very aware of personal shortcomings. We are all works in progress and all know these areas in which we need His grace to enable and empower us to live as He desires. If the reality is that we reproduce who we are and not just who we want to be, then we need to get it right and move forward in that process of becoming more like Christ. We need to ask ourselves the question, "Am I ashamed of my private world? Do I fear what others might see when my guard is down?"

I am sure that many will have heard of Bob Mumford's "mumps and measles" illustration. It goes something like this: I catch mumps – a nasty case of mumps! I come to you and I warn you, "Hey, be careful... I have measles. They are really nasty and now you have spent time with me you might catch measles too!" Measles... measles... measles! I go on and on about measles. I go to great lengths to tell you about the fact that I have them, I describe to you in detail the symptoms and the way I feel as a result of having measles. So, after a few weeks I bump into you again and it is no surprise that you have caught... the mumps!

It is the very same principle when it comes to reproducing our lives in others. The fruit that we reproduce in others is the fruit that we are bearing in our own lives... not the fruit we would like to have, or even pretend to have. With the mentoring process there is an *impartation* that takes place; it is not just a teaching-based programme but rather a *demonstration* through our lifestyle. It is for this reason that we must be wise in how we choose our leaders. We need to ask ourselves, "What fruit will she reproduce in the lives of others?" We are not looking for "gifting" or ability, but a godly character. *Remember – you can teach what you know but you reproduce who you are!*

> A good tree cannot bring forth evil fruits, nor can a corrupt tree bring forth good fruit.
>
> (Matthew 7:18, MKJV)

4. A Woman Who has Learnt to Dwell in the Higher Places When the Storm Rages

Life is messy. It has a habit of creeping up from behind and just dumping us, like those massive waves in the ocean. You see it coming and hope to ride it but somehow the timing is not quite right and you suddenly find yourself face down, coughing up mouthfuls of sand and wondering how on earth you got there! Does that sound familiar?

There is much in life that we can not anticipate, prepare for, or avoid – it is just suddenly upon us. It is in these moments that we are faced with a choice. It happens quickly and we need to be quick to discern it but we need to decide in that moment whether we are going to live *under* the circumstance or *above* the circumstance. If we are constantly dictated to by what life throws at us, we will live in a place of turmoil, endlessly tossed about on the waves of life. This produces instability in us, a lifestyle full of ups and downs and highs and lows, depending on how life is treating us. Maturity comes when we are able, through His empowering grace, to rise above that which is taking place in the physical and to gain a godly perspective.

Let us be honest here. Generally speaking we, as women, are emotional creatures. Add the dreaded hormones into the mix and we have a recipe for disaster! As mature women of God, we need to be able to make good choices in the middle of difficult circumstances. However much those hormones are raging we can still choose how we are going to respond in the heat of the moment. However out of control we may feel, we can still decide whether we are going to give in to our emotions, or choose to exercise the fruit of self-control (Galatians 5:23). We must learn in these times to step back from the intensity of the moment and to cry out to Him for the strength to walk in obedience.

Of course, this principle applies to every area of life. A few months ago, God gave me a picture during one of the Sunday morning celebrations. I was looking upwards and it was as if a small rope ladder was lowered from heaven and His voice said, "Come. Climb up to the higher places with me and I will show you another perspective." In difficult times and seasons in our lives we must learn to dwell in the higher places; it is from this place that we can gain a clear perspective of what is really going on. It is from here that we can hear Him whisper His words of love and reassurance into our souls. It is from here that secrets from Father to daughter and daughter to Father can be exchanged and we receive the strength to carry on. To

endure means *to outlast the problem* and this can only be
achieved by walking closely with Him.

In the middle of trials and difficulties we can easily lose
our way. Not long ago, our family joined with some friends
for a day out at Leeds Castle. In the grounds of the castle
they have a maze, and the children and some of the adults
decided to go in. Neil stood outside on a grassy mound,
from where he could see the whole maze from a higher
perspective. I went in and, needless to say, got totally lost!
I kept running in all directions, each time sure that this
was the right way, only to find myself at another dead end.
Eventually I called to Neil and he came and lifted me up
over the hedges so I could get a higher perspective, just as
he had had when he had been standing watching the whole
comical scene. From higher up, it all looked so easy and
straightforward; I could see exactly where I needed to go.
We then began to shout directions to the others so that they
too could find their way.

It is the same in our Christian walk. The closer we draw
to God in the difficult times the *greater* He becomes and
the *smaller* our problems or difficulties appear. When He
is magnified, everything else shrinks back to its accurate
size. We must remember that we are 'Throne Room People'.
We are seated in heavenly places with Christ.

> But God, who is rich in mercy, because of His great
> love with which He loved us, even when we were
> dead in trespasses, made us alive together with
> Christ (by grace you have been saved), and raised
> us up together, and made us sit together in the
> heavenly places in Christ Jesus...
>
> (Ephesians 2:4–6, NKJV)

This is the awesome truth of His Word. From the throne room, mountains begin to look like molehills and we can gain a godly perspective. We need, like David, to speak to our souls in the tough times rather than listen to them; our souls tend to lie to us during the difficult times.

> Why are you cast down, O my soul?
> And why are you disquieted within me?
> *Hope in God*, for I shall yet praise Him
> For the help of His countenance.
> O my God, my soul is cast down within me;
> Therefore I will remember you...

> (Psalm 42:5–6, NKJV, my italics)

As you read through this psalm, you see that poor David was really going through it. Yet he chose to speak to his soul rather than just listen to it. He tells his soul to *hope in God* and to *praise Him* despite what he is feeling and experiencing. He reminds himself of how God has always come through for him in the past, he holds on to what he knows to be true when life and circumstances appear to contradict it. He knows his God intimately and therefore is able to trust Him despite what he is seeing take place in the physical.

We will dwell in the places that we allow our minds to take us. Therefore we must be disciplined in what we allow ourselves to meditate upon and be quick to take all thoughts, feelings and emotions captive to the obedience of Christ. I am not suggesting that we become so heavenly minded that we are of no earthly good; dwelling in the higher places does not mean we lose a grip on reality and bury our heads in the sand, tempting as it may be at times! It is being able to see "reality" clearly, from a godly perspective rather than from an entirely physical one.

5. A Woman Who is Busy About Her Father's Business

She opens her mouth in skillful and godly Wisdom, and on her tongue is the law of kindness [giving counsel and instruction]. She looks well to how things go in her household, and the bread of idleness (gossip, discontent, and self-pity) she will not eat.

(Proverbs 31:26–27, AMPLIFIED BIBLE)

Because it is not merely a teaching or giving of information that occurs through the mentoring but an impartation, it is essential that our leaders are living godly lifestyles and that they are productive in their busyness. We need to put a guard over our mouths and not speak unkindly about others. This passage in Proverbs 31 warns us not to eat the bread of idleness. In the Amplified version it gives us a further insight into what idleness consists of: gossip, discontent and self-pity. These three areas can often entrap us as women. Let us take a look at each one of these.

Gossip

There can be a tendency in women to have an unhealthy appetite for the nitty-gritty of others' lives. We love to know the details – the good... but also the bad! Maybe a part of us wants to compare ourselves, or maybe we are just curious, but the Word makes it very clear that we are not to be gossips or busybodies (2 Corinthians 12:20).

To gossip about others shows a lack of maturity on our part and often reveals our own insecurities. Gossip is destructive and has an immediate impact on at least three lives – the person gossiping, the person being gossiped to and the person being gossiped about. A gossip is quick to pass on information, regardless of how destructive it may be. The sobering fact is that if they say things *to* you, you can be pretty sure that they will say things *about* you, too! They cannot be trusted and end up with poor reputations and few friends. We need to be careful that we do not speak negatively about others.

In a group context, it can be very difficult to get to the source of gossip as it weaves many threads. When Michael and Heather were leading a youth group this became a bit of an issue but it was hard to expose the individuals who were at the heart of it. Michael decided to get all the young people together and gave them each a Scripture about gossip to look up. There are hundreds of them! They each had to read their verse out to the rest of the group and then Michael said, "OK... now you know what the Word of God says on gossip and you are playing a dangerous game." It cut the thing dead and broke the pattern in these youngsters' lives. The fear of God hit them and they stepped up to a new level of holiness.

Gossip can be a weakness if we struggle in the area of fear of man, or if we are too concerned with what others think about us. Jesus wants to free us from an unhealthy need to be accepted on these terms and to cultivate within our hearts a greater fear of God than of people. Our words and what we speak over others can be powerful. We need to be careful of what we say, particularly in those times when our guard may be down and we are vulnerable. If we have been hurt or offended by somebody, we may feel the need to complain to someone else and think we are totally justified in doing so – but be careful; the fact is that gossip is sin. We must not allow our feelings of hurt to turn inwards and become destructive, however entitled we may feel to own those feelings. Forgiveness gives the Holy Spirit room to bring healing and restoration to our hearts and prevents us from growing bitter or resentful. If we can walk a lifestyle of forgiveness, we will be less likely to gossip or speak negatively about others.

Gossip can be very subtle and we may not even be aware that we are in the habit of practising it. Ask the Holy Spirit to heighten your awareness and to shine His light into any areas that may be blind spots. I have found it helpful in my own life to ask myself these three questions before I open my mouth: Is it good? Is it kind? Is it necessary? If the answer is "no" to any of these then I keep quiet and choose to say nothing. To begin with it may take discipline and effort but you will be surprised how quickly old habits can be broken and new ones established. As His daughters, we want our lives to radiate Him and our words to be full of kindness and love.

Discontent

Discontent is a tool of the enemy that draws us far away from the goodness and kindness of God. It warps our understanding of the nature and character of our heavenly Father and it can eat away at our souls. It is destructive and feeds upon any part of "self" that has not been fully crucified with Christ. I have met people who are so bound by discontent that they are unable to be pleased for others when things go well for them. They resent anyone who has what they do not have and are full of envy and bitterness.

They are filled with an insatiable craving for more and see no pleasure in that which they are already blessed to have. All joy is stolen when we live in a place of discontent. It is so important for us to learn to be content – with or without.

> Not that I speak in regard to need, for I have learned in whatever state I am, to be content: I know how to be abased, and I know how to abound. Everywhere and in all things I have learned both to be full and to be hungry, both to abound and to suffer need. I can do all things through Christ who strengthens me.
>
> (Philippians 4:11–13, NKJV)

To live in a place of contentment is not necessarily something that comes naturally to us, for we are constantly at war with our flesh (Romans 7:13–25), but it is a place that we can learn to dwell in. The key is to starve feelings of discontent rather than feed them. If we allow these feelings to grow in us, discontent can take a hold and cause our hearts to harden; let us not be tempted to eat of its fruit.

One of the greatest tools that the enemy will use to create discontent with our circumstances, belongings or lifestyles, is to cause us to compare ourselves with others. When we are tempted to focus on what others have, we lay ourselves wide open for the devil to come in and stir up discontent in our hearts. We need to constantly refocus and look at things through God's eyes in order to gain a clear perspective.

One area worth addressing briefly is the whole minefield of money and materialism. Jesus warns us clearly and firmly in His Word regarding the dangers of money and the love of it. As soon as we slip into the trap of desiring and longing for nice things and material possessions, we become susceptible to the pull of the world. The world is forever pushing the "have it because you deserve it" mentality and there is the constant pressure to keep up with the Joneses.

A good leveller here is the statement "Live simply so that others might simply live". I am not suggesting that as Christians we are to have a poverty mentality, or that it is wrong to have material possessions. As in everything, however, we need to maintain a godly perspective and hold lightly that which He has blessed us with. We will all have to give an account one day for how we have used that which He has entrusted to us. Paul says, "I can do all things through Christ who strengthens me" (Philippians 4:13, NKJV). Herein lies the secret to being content; the power of Christ at work in our hearts, changing us, moulding us, and keeping us strong in His mighty strength.

Self-pity

We can all admit to times when we have given in to self-pity but just seeing it for what it is should help us to run from it as fast as possible. Like discontent, it is rooted in self and, as much as it may comfort our flesh, it is like a destructive poison to our spirits. Jim McNally, in his book, *Sonship: The Path to Fatherhood*, says the following about self-pity:

> The origin of self pity is to question the goodness of God. To indulge in self pity is an ungodly response, because it judges circumstances by their effect upon ones self. A person in self pity will see all suffering as evil. The Bible has nothing good to say about pouting, grumbling or complaining. When

fathers allow their children to indulge in self pity
they promote a victim mentality.[1]

Self-pity loves to gather friends. Often not content to indulge
alone, we search for others who will come alongside us
and join our pity parties. We huddle together and compare
notes on who has the saddest story to tell, breeding the
spirit of "poor me" and "it's not fair". At Jubilee Church, we
refer to this as "feeding one another's monkeys". There is a
spiritual dynamic that occurs as we make agreements with
one another and, as we do so, we give the enemy access to
stir up our misery and despair. If we give in to self-pity it
can literally "take us out" for extensive periods of time and
cause us to become completely ineffective in our Christian
service.

As I mentioned earlier, when I was eighteen, I was blessed
to have a godly mentor who spoke into my life. Now, over
twenty years later, Pat Cook and I still meet regularly and
she still asks me the hard questions! I am so grateful for
her input in my life and for all the wisdom, patience and
friendship she has given to me.

On one of the first times we met together, I remember
being very self-absorbed, as many teenagers are today. We
sat down in her lounge and I began to pour out my heart.
The list of "problems" was quite long; so much can happen
in a week as a teenager! I had expected an ear to listen and
a shoulder to cry on. What I actually got sent me reeling
and I still remember it to this day: "Hazel, self-pity is not a
luxury we can afford as Christians, so just get over it."

I was shocked! Where was my hug? Where was my
"There, there, poor you!"? Instead, she quickly pointed out
the error of my ways and helped me to see just how ugly
self-pity was! I am so thankful for the painful lesson that I

learned that day. I have never forgotten it and have passed it on to many a poor and unsuspecting person since! In my own life, self-pity is an area in which I am learning to become brutal and I am realizing that total intolerance is the only way to rid ourselves of it. We must abandon ourselves to the mercy of Christ and run into His arms for the comfort that we need.

Dee Harris, a leader in Valley Christian Church, Fishhoek, once shared a very challenging story. She had been away and got back to discover that her home had been burgled. They had taken everything, including very personal items, and she was devastated by her loss. She walked out of the house and went to the beach to let out her grief. In recalling the story she made this statement: "... I said to myself, Dee, you can have ten minutes to complain and then you must move on. God is still God." I remember thinking, "Ten minutes! I would need ten years!" She was not willing to give self-pity an inch and neither should we.

It never ceases to amaze me how my children never miss a beat; they see everything, and it is much the same in leadership. Those we lead are watching us. They will quickly spot those areas that have not been yielded to the Lordship of Christ. We lead by our example and therefore we cannot afford to be a part of that which is contrary to the will of God. Gossip, discontent and self-pity are all fruits of idleness in our lives and, if we are busy about our Father's business, there should be no room for them. Partaking in these things not only disqualifies us and gives the enemy an open door into our hearts but they also cause others to stumble.

We put no stumbling block in anyone's path, so that our ministry will not be discredited.

(2 Corinthians 6:3, NIV)

As daughters of the King, with plans and purposes to fulfil, we do not have time to sit and eat the bread of idleness. Rather, we should be feeding upon Him – the Bread of Life, a source that not only sustains us but others too. Eating of the bread of idleness will seriously stunt our growth as Christians but eating of the Bread of Life will nourish us and lead us into green pastures, a far more pleasant place than a pity party to invite others to come and join us! Eating and feasting on the Bread of Life is a critical part of living life big.

> "Most assuredly, I say to you, Moses did not give you the bread from heaven, but My Father gives you the true bread from heaven. For the bread of God is He who comes down from heaven and gives life to the world." Then they said to Him, "Lord give us this bread always." And Jesus said to them, "I am the bread of life. He who comes to Me shall never hunger, and he who believes in Me shall never thirst."

(John 6:32–35, NKJV)

He must be our source, the place we draw from to satisfy the hunger in our hearts and the thirst in our spirits.

When so much of our time is poured into the lives of others, it is essential that He remains our source and sustainer. Giving of ourselves, however great our personal capacity, cannot be maintained indefinitely but in Him there is *always* enough. He never runs dry. He never becomes weary. He is always at the peak of His power!

6. A Woman Who Knows Her True Identity

This is my Son, whom I love; with him I am well
pleased.

(Matthew 3:17, NIV)

It always fascinates me that God said this before Jesus had
done anything remarkable. It was before He had performed
miracles, cast out demons or turned water into wine. It was
before He had forgiven any sinners or raised anyone from
the dead. God was reaffirming His heart of total love and
acceptance, as a Father to a Son. He was establishing here
the fact that Jesus was loved, accepted, and the true Son of
the living God. It was an unconditional love, based on *who*
Jesus was rather than what He would do or later become.

Before Jesus had "done" anything, He was confident in
the knowledge that He was His Father's Son, He was loved
by Him unconditionally and that His Dad was pleased with
Him. It was in this moment, just before Christ embarked on
His ministry, that Jesus publicly received love, acceptance
and an establishing of His true and undeniable identity:
Jesus Christ, Son of the living God!

To lead others in the Lord we must have that inner
confidence and assurance of who we are and to whom
we belong, where our true identity lies. This needs to
be settled in our minds *before* we enter into any form of
ministry or leadership so that we can operate from a place
of wholeness rather than from a place of insecurity, self-
doubt or performance-based leadership.

The need to belong is within each one of us. We have
been designed that way. And yet so many of us, even those
who have been Christians for years, have never had this

revelation that totally changes our hearts for ever. Do you still have that ache deep within, that longing to belong and feel accepted? Then maybe you have not had your eyes and hearts opened to the truth of who you really are in Christ Jesus. When we fail to see this incredible truth that we are His, bought at a price and loved unconditionally, then we live with a constant restlessness and lack of inner peace.

It is only in the last few years that I have really begun to grasp this truth in my own life, and those who know me will testify that the change it has made has left me almost unrecognizable from the person I once was. They say, "You look different, you act differently, you even talk differently." I realize that so many of the fears and insecurities I lived with were all just symptoms of this one underlying factor – I did not *know* that I was unconditionally loved and accepted.

I have come to see and understand that despite the rejection I may have suffered at the hands of others, my worth, value and identity can remain unshaken. No one can take away from me the fact that I am my Father's daughter. This truth has become an unshakable foundation upon which all else is built. My prayer for each one of you is this:

> that the God of our Lord Jesus Christ, the Father
> of glory, may give to you the spirit of wisdom and
> revelation in the knowledge of Him, the eyes of your
> understanding being enlightened...
>
> (Ephesians 1:17–18, NKJV)

The Spirit opens our eyes to the truth that the enemy so desperately wants to keep hidden from us. Do you struggle to grasp this profound truth, that you are His? If so, pray for the spirit of revelation to bring you into this knowledge of Him, your Father, whose arms are waiting to embrace you.

So often, our need to be needed is rooted in a lack of understanding of who we are in Christ. We try to find our worth and value in so many things; our jobs, ministries, being a good wife and mother, sport, physical looks and appearance and financial security to name but a few. But all these things are subject to change. However tightly we may try to hold on to them, they have a habit of slipping through our fingers. In losing our grip we often lose our sense of value and worth too, leaving us spluttering and fighting to stay afloat. A striving and a need to prove ourselves can then drive us, rather than being able to just rest in the knowledge of who we are in Christ.

When it comes to mentoring others, we need to be fully persuaded that we know our identity in Christ. Otherwise, our motivation can come from a "need to be needed" basis, instead of a desire to produce good fruit in others. Rather than pointing others to Jesus, we can be tempted to set ourselves up as their "strong tower" because in doing so, a need is met in us. This is dangerous because we do not actually have what they need and we are not able to be the answer to their problems – Jesus is! Only in Jesus can they find what they are looking for. Our aim is to point them to Jesus, not ourselves.

I remember a lady once phoned me in real distress. She sounded so desperate – the need was apparently urgent. I was about to invite her round for a coffee and a shoulder to cry on when I felt a check in my spirit. "Teach her to run to Me first," I heard the Holy Spirit whisper. I let her talk and then said, "Now go and tell your Father all that you have just told me. Pour your heart out to Him and then listen to what He has to say to you. I will be praying for you while you do this. Phone me later and let me know how it goes."

She went and did what I had suggested and had a real encounter with her Father God. She met with Him on such a deep level and received a healing and restoration I could never have given her.

When our motivation in mentoring becomes about meeting a need in us, we will reproduce this in others too. Before you know it, Jesus is taken out of the picture and it just becomes about self-gratification and causing others to be dependent upon us. Good leadership is not about making ourselves irreplaceable in the lives of others, it is about equipping them to find all they need in Jesus. We need to be regularly checking our hearts in this area and be quick to repent when we see that our motives are ungodly. A healthy, biblical self-image prevents a defensive attitude and protects us from being easily hurt or offended. By "biblical self-image" I mean a clear understanding of our identity and worth being founded in Christ alone. I knew a lady who was a gifted counsellor. She was very experienced and helped many people through difficult and traumatic issues. However, due to unresolved issues in her life, she found that spending time with needy individuals met a need in her. Consequently, there developed an unhealthy dependency between both parties. Instead of leading people to a place of freedom, she attempted to carry their burdens and ended up burned out.

7. A Woman Who Carries a Heart for Other Ladies

This may well seem an obvious quality necessary in a mentoring leader but it is important to ensure that it is evident. Let us look at our definition of mentoring:

> Mentoring is a relational experience, through which one person empowers another by sharing God-given resources.

> *Paul Stanley and Robert Clinton*

Part of the mentoring process is about making rich deposits into the lives of those we are walking with; we can only do this effectively if we are passionate about them. To mentor another person, we need to be relational. This may not be a natural part of our make-up but I believe it is something God gives to those who eagerly desire it. Looking to Jesus as our model, we see that He was relational to the core, a lover of people. As His daughters, I am confident that we all carry a measure of this relational quality because we have been made in His image.

The ability to see their God-given potential is also essential. We are not just assessing where they are at but also where they could potentially be. We need vision and the ability to look ahead and suggest the next step. We believe not just in who they are but who they can become in Christ. Of course, it cannot be our sole responsibility to make sure they reach their potential. They also need to strongly desire it, cry out for it, fight for it, and be willing to pay the price for it! Often the things that prevent us from reaching our potential are those blind spots in our lives. Who is there that cares enough to lovingly point out our weaknesses and confront the things that disqualify us from achieving our true potential? This is part of the role of a good mentor.

When Jesus chose His twelve men, He not only recognized their inadequacy but He also saw their potential. Peter, the rock, who would be instrumental in building His church; John, the beloved, into whose care He entrusted His own mother; Thomas, the doubter, whose fingers needed to touch the wounds before he could believe. Jesus knew these men so well, was painfully aware of their weaknesses and shortcomings, and yet remained in their company for three years. He knew not only who they were, but more importantly, what they would one day become. He believed in them and He saw the transition they made as they followed His example. What quicker way is there to facilitate growth in the life of an individual than to demonstrate by lifestyle? John Maxwell, in *Becoming a Person of Influence*, says the following:

> The mentoring process offers people the
> opportunity to turn their potential into reality,
> their dreams into destiny. Mentors impact eternity
> because there is no telling where their influence
> will stop.[2]

If our heart is to enlarge the potential and growth in the lives of others, then it is vital that we too are enlarging and growing in our personal lives. We need to be continually returning to the source, Jesus Christ, to receive from Him all we need – both for ourselves and those He has entrusted to our care. Proverbs is packed full of wisdom and advice for living. Look at this little nugget:

> There is one who scatters,
> yet increases more;

And there is one who withholds more than is right,
But it leads to poverty.
The generous soul will be made rich,
And he who waters will also be watered himself.

(Proverbs 11:24–25, NKJV)

God has spoken to me so much through these verses. I believe God has put in each one of us that which is not only for our benefit but also for the benefit of others. Much of what we walk through in life is for a greater purpose. We have the privilege of imparting to others that which we have learned through the tough times and through the trials of life. There is an enriching and an increase that takes place on a spiritual level when we do this.

...there is one who scatters, yet increases more...

In the same way, when we withhold from freely giving that which He has given to us, there is a spiritual stunting or poverty that takes place.

... there is one who withholds more than is right,
But it leads to poverty...

There are times in ministry when we reach what we think is our limit. "God, I cannot give any more, I have nothing left to give." This happens in those busy seasons in my life when I have neglected to draw from Him as my source and consequently have been giving out of my lack. Eventually, I go into self-preservation mode and put up little fences to protect myself from burnout and exhaustion. However, although my plan is to find some peace and quiet from the storm, what seems to happen is that I enter into a place of spiritual poverty. Why? I am trying to hold onto and preserve that which should be given away. The promise comes in verse 25:

> ... the generous soul will be made rich,
> And he who waters will also be watered himself.

There is a richness of blessing that comes in our giving and there is a watering for our souls as we water others. At the beginning of this chapter we have the quote:

> A single candle can light a thousand more without diminishing itself.

This is what happens when we are flowing out of the fullness of what He has poured into our lives. You see, on our own we cannot sustain the demands and needs of others; we were never designed to do so. We are His vessels, here to carry His love to a broken world. It is not our love that they need but His love manifest in us. His love never runs dry, and in Him there is always enough.

Those who are naturally empathetic or pastoral are particularly vulnerable in this area. They must guard against carrying others' burdens and as a result becoming ineffective in moving them forward to a place of wholeness. As mentors, our role is not one of carrying their problems or taking their burdens from them but one of equipping them so that they can grow and become mature, complete, lacking nothing!

In the same way that steel is tempered, God allows hardship and adversity to help the maturing process. Therefore offering others a quick way out of their difficulty may not always be the best solution. We want to see them enlarged through the process and to stand with them to see their personal victories and deliverance. Let me give you a simple example.

One of our ladies was recently asked to give her testimony at our annual ladies' mentoring banquet. She declined the offer without any thought. She was terrified and felt it would be too much for her. Her mentor had a choice – to accept her quick answer or to challenge her to push through. She was encouraged and challenged to go ahead and give her testimony. In spite of those very real feelings of fear and nervousness, she rose to the challenge and shared from the heart. Standing there, in front of nearly seventy people, her mentor close by her side, she shared a powerful testimony and achieved a personal victory. Not only that, but many other lives were challenged and impacted by what she shared. We need to ensure that we do not miss those little opportunities in life in which growth can naturally occur in our hearts. So often we want to cover, nurture and protect as soon as we see someone having a hard time. Of course, there are specific seasons in life where this plays a vital role in healing and restoration. But our responsibility is also to equip these ladies to be overcomers who know how to push through in those areas that hold them captive.

8. A Woman Who Walks in Accountability in Her Own Life

It is very important if you are mentoring others to ensure that you have someone, or several people, to whom you are submitted and with whom you make yourself accountable.

Let me mention here that if you are considering starting up a mentoring programme in your church, you need to have the full support and blessing of your leadership. Go to them and submit your thoughts and ideas before embarking on something on your own. It is foolish and unwise to set up anything without first gaining your leadership team's full support. If you try to operate outside of their covering, you lay yourself wide open to the enemy and he will take you out one way or another! What is birthed in rebellion can never receive God's approval. God has appointed godly leaders over you for your protection, and submission to them is essential if the desire is to succeed and bear good fruit. I find it helpful to consider my leadership as an umbrella of protection. All the time I remain under the umbrella, I am sheltered, protected and can work effectively in God's kingdom without making myself vulnerable to the enemy.

Accountability is what we expect from the ladies who commit to the mentoring programme and from those who have been appointed as leaders. We all need someone to ask us the hard questions, to hold us to account for the things we have said we would do and to check up on us regularly. This is not about control or domination but rather a means of protecting and lovingly covering one another. We can make ourselves accountable to numerous people but unless we are prepared to open our lives to them and be totally honest, we do both them and ourselves a huge disservice. It is not enough to say, "Please can I be accountable to you?" if we are not willing to be truthful with those secret and sometimes shameful areas of our lives. A relationship that provides accountability should be a safe and secure place. Reading his letters, it is obvious that the apostle Paul knew intimate details about Timothy's character and lifestyle, but Timothy felt affirmed and loved by Paul. I am convinced it is this safe and secure accountable relationship that helped Timothy to reach his potential in Christ and protected him from some of the pitfalls that befell his contemporaries.

To mentor others, we need to be living within godly

boundaries and disciplines. We also need someone who will speak honestly into our lives and point out those areas to which we may be blind. Proverbs 27:6 reminds us that, "Faithful are the wounds of a friend, But the kisses of an enemy are deceitful." When someone corrects you, how do you respond? There are those who react and become defensive and there are those who embrace the correction, process it and allow the power of the Holy Spirit to transform them. Which one sounds more like you? Of course, the admonishment must be done in love and through relationship and trust but that is why *you* choose your accountable relationships. Don't pick your greatest fan! Be wise and choose someone who will be honest with you, even when it hurts. As mentors, we cannot expect others to make themselves accountable to us if we are not willing to walk in accountability in our own lives.

In the next chapter, we see how godly boundaries are put in place.

NOTES

1 Jim McNally, *Sonship: The Path to Fatherhood*, published privately.

2 John Maxwell, Jim Dornan, *Becoming a Person of Influence*, Nashville, Tennessee: Thomas Nelson Publishers, 1997.

10

Is That Your Boot Up My Butt?

Love and Godly Boundaries

by Heather

Sometimes your medicine bottle has on it, "shake well before using". That is what God has to do with some of His people. He has to shake them well before they are ever useable.

Unknown

Shaking usually serves one of two purposes. Firstly, pharmacists often mix liquids with powders as they prepare potent medicines and it is only when they are shaken before being used that they serve any purpose. The world as we knew it experienced a shaking on 11 September 2001 and never before have I witnessed a more powerful demonstration of complete strangers coming together to form an "impenetrable front". However, there are also times when shaking causes separation. When sifting for gold beside a river there is a lot that goes into that sifting tray, precious little of which is actually gold!

It is only as the tray is shaken that the sand and dirt are sifted away, leaving behind precious gold.

Being shaken by God is never easy and certainly not comfortable. I have experienced both types of shaking in my life; shaking with the purpose of being united and also shaking to break off the dead branches. A member of my family recently walked a really difficult testing road; a shaking that none of us could have predicted. I know that through this situation, we came together as a family and, as a result, now enjoy a far deeper level of relationship and transparency with one another. Then there have been the times where I have experienced a shaking from God as He, through His great love for me, has sifted away fears and insecurities, leaving behind His intents and purposes for my life.

I have always seen it as such an incredible privilege to have the opportunity to walk with someone as they journey through life and it is certainly not a responsibility that I take lightly. I have seen how God has worked in the lives of individuals, gently shaking in order to bring about lasting change. He is so faithful and the thing that I have realized over and over again is that He knows what He is doing; we *can* trust Him, because of His incredible love for us. He knows us much more intimately than we even know ourselves and we need to remember that He is always able to see the bigger picture.

So, what exactly is our responsibility when it comes to the lives of others? In Genesis 4, we pick up on the story where Cain had just killed his brother, Abel. God questioned Cain regarding his brother, to which Cain responded with a question. It is a question that I have also asked and pondered on: "Am I my brother's keeper?"

I have to smile when I think of this story, because

although none of the people I have walked with have ever ended up murdering anyone, the root issues that I have seen in peoples' lives are pretty similar. What had happened just prior to Abel's death? These brothers were hard-working young men; one saw to the animals while the other farmed. One day, they both presented an offering to God; Abel sacrificed one of the firstborn of the flock while Cain's offering is described as "fruits of the soil" (Genesis 4:3, NIV). There was a problem, though, at least for Cain, because God looked favourably upon Abel's sacrifice but unfavourably upon Cain's. This made Cain extremely *angry* and *jealous*. So what did God do? We read that God addressed Cain's bad attitude with a warning of how it could potentially lead him further astray.

We always need to remember in life that it's not what happens to us, *but how we respond* that counts. It was not only Cain's sacrifice that God was addressing:

> Then the Lord said to Cain, "Why are you angry? Why is your face downcast? If you do what is right, will you not be accepted? But if you do not do what is right, *sin is crouching at your door; it desires to have you, but you must master it.*
>
> (Genesis 4:6–7, NIV, my italics)

A bad attitude can still be nipped in the bud; left unchecked it could lead to deeper issues.

Going back to the question, then, what does it mean to be your brother's keeper? Where does our responsibility start and end regarding choices that people make in their lives? Petty jealousy and anger, similar issues to those faced by Cain, are rife in many churches today and I believe that as leaders we are faced with a choice. Firstly, we could hold the opinion that each person is responsible before God for his/her own actions and attitudes. It is so much easier to live in harmony in the body of Christ without the potential strife of having to get people to try to change their ways. We could simply look the other way and get on with the business that we have been called to.

Or the alternative, motivated by our love for the people and a desire to see them being used effectively in the kingdom and walking in wholeness, is to address bad attitudes, sometimes even doing this at the risk of personal rejection. When David wrote Psalm 23, he understood that *comfort for our souls* is only brought about when a sympathetic shoulder goes hand in hand with "a boot up our butts"! In other words, we have an opportunity to grow in maturity when we are able to learn from our mistakes with the support of close friends and leaders who care enough about us to confront the glaring issues in our lives.

Your rod *and* Your staff, they comfort me.

(Psalm 23:4b, NKJV)

Part 1: God's Staff

My parents, in South Africa, bought and moved to a new farm. My father had previously farmed with vegetables but decided that at the age of sixty-five a change would be good. While we were thinking it might be a good time for him to start considering retirement, he was thinking about farming with cattle! He is still busy developing the infrastructure of his new farm by putting up fences and building roads but in the meantime he has bought ducks, geese, chickens, a horse called Jessie, and some sheep. Our recent visit to the farm was to attend a family reunion where we celebrated Christmas together for the first time in ten years.

You can imagine our excitement the day after Christmas when the news reached us that one of my dad's ewes had just given birth to the cutest little lamb you have ever seen. Keeping to the Christmas theme, we named her Carol. The drama continued as we realized that the poor mother was still moaning and groaning and that perhaps there was another one still inside! Fortunately, my brother's mother-in-law used to be a midwife; so, on went the gloves and into the field we all trekked – eight curious and very brave children and about seven anxious adults. It was soon evident that the second lamb would be stillborn but we decided that the children could continue to look as the biology lesson had now turned into a lesson about life and death. (My niece, aged six, had to leave when we noticed she was turning white and starting to perspire!) Our midwife managed to deliver the second little lamb, which we then buried. Despite a few tears, we were thrilled that at least the mother still had little Carol who by this stage was doing very well indeed.

What surprised me in this whole episode was how difficult it is to catch a sheep – even one that has just given birth and is still in labour. They are very fast, very strong animals and, in order to work with them, you need to first catch them and then hold them down very firmly so that they cannot run away. That pretty much sums up my first-hand knowledge of sheep; I cannot imagine being a shepherd and having a whole flock of them to look after! It is one thing to lead them to good grazing but what does a shepherd do if they get sick?

This is where his staff comes in handy. A staff is a straight stick, about six feet long and curved at one end into the shape of a hook. Shepherds are constantly on the lookout for either water or greener pastures and are thus always exploring new territory. A shepherd can use his staff to help him climb over rocks to survey their stability before leading his sheep there. He can also use it to check out crevices and caves for snakes and scorpions that could harm his sheep. For centuries, the shepherd's staff has been recognized as an instrument of *guidance* and *restraint*. For example, the crook can be slipped around a sheep's neck to restrain it or guide it, or even stop it from fighting or falling. The shepherd also uses his staff to communicate with his sheep – a tap on the hind leg will bring a sheep back into position, while a tap on the head of the lead sheep makes it lie down so that the others will follow.

You may at this point be wondering about the relevance of a lesson on sheep. I mentioned earlier that in Psalm 23:4b, David writes about the rod and staff, working *together* to bring comfort to us.

> The Lord is my shepherd, I shall not be in want.
> He *makes* me lie down in green pastures,
> he leads me beside quiet waters,
> he restores my soul.
> He guides me in paths of righteousness
> for his name's sake.

(Psalm 23:1–3, NIV)

Isaiah also compares the Sovereign Lord to a shepherd when he says:

> He tends His flock like a shepherd:
> He gathers the lambs in his arms
> and carries them close to his heart;
> he gently leads those that have young.

(Isaiah 40:11, NIV)

What a precious picture of our Father's heart towards His children. So how then does all this apply to us? In the New Testament, the Greek word for "shepherd" is *poimen*. It carries the understanding of a herdsman, one who tends, watches over and shares his life with the sheep. Peter urges us to "Be shepherds of God's flock that is under your care, serving as overseers – not because you must, but because you are willing, as God wants you to be" (1 Peter 5:2, NIV). Later, Peter goes on to describe Jesus as our *archipoimen*, our Chief Shepherd (1 Peter 5:4, NIV). It is vital that we, as His 'under' shepherds, imitate Jesus as the Good Shepherd (John 10:11, NIV).

Role of the Shepherd

Think back on what you have already read about how shepherds use their crooks or staffs. For the following five points, I have used key words from Ezekiel 34 to more clearly define the role of the shepherd within the church context.

1. Being a shepherd means that we *nurture* those whom God has entrusted to us. This means that we know them well enough to understand what makes them tick. On a practical note, this involves making regular contact with them through either visiting them, or phoning them, by sending a card, or by sending them a text. It means being there for them during difficult times. This could be in the form of organizing meals for them, or picking up their children from school. It could also mean making time to just listen – to *really listen* to them. It is about showing the practical love of Jesus to those around us. Kate is a young mother and also one of our mentoring leaders in

Jubilee. She recently shared a testimony about a time where she felt the Lord prompt her to buy some flowers for an elderly neighbour. She did not know the lady at all but was obedient and bought a bouquet. However, when she arrived at the lady's house to deliver the flowers, she noticed through the window that the lady was asleep on her sofa. She decided not to disturb her. A couple of days later (when Kate realized that the flowers were not going to last for ever!) she had an opportunity to deliver the flowers again, but this time there were guests at the lady's house. She knocked on the door and rather sheepishly gave her the flowers, saying that they were a gift. The lady was overwhelmed by her kindness. Kate did not want to disturb her and her visitors, so she left. You can imagine Kate's surprise when, talking to the lady a few days later, she found out that it had been her birthday on the day that Kate had delivered the flowers. God's timing is always perfect! The lady was so blessed and is now completely open for Kate to begin to build a friendship with her.

2. Shepherding means that we help to *lead them to greener pastures*. Shepherds many years ago used to actually *lead* the sheep, walking in front with the flock following behind. If we are shepherding God's people, we need to make sure that we are walking in front, leaving a path that is safe for them to follow. I love the old proverb that goes like this: "If you think you're leading and no one is following you, then you're only going for a walk!"

It is important when shepherding someone that we make sure they are being properly *nourished*.

> Man does not live on bread alone, but on every word that comes from the mouth of God.
>
> *(Matthew 4:4, NIV)*

Are we encouraging them to spend more time in God's Word and, where possible, are we helping them to understand the Scriptures and how to apply them to their lives? There are so many excellent equipping resources (books, teaching DVDs) available to us today and we need to make sure that we are equipping, leading and guiding those whom God has placed in our care. This is not so that they become dependent upon us but to ensure that we are constantly pointing them in the direction of our Chief Shepherd.

David, in Psalm 23, describes how our Shepherd leads us beside still waters. I believe it is so important that we are aware of people who seem constantly frazzled by their busy lifestyles. We need time to reflect and take stock of our lives and unless we actively pursue quiet times in our lives, believe me, it will never happen. My father-in-law, Derek Puffett, loves to go camping in the Pilansberg Game Reserve in South Africa. He regularly packs up his little tent and goes off on his own at least once a quarter for a couple of days at a time. He always testifies to the fact that he feels refreshed and re-envisioned on his return to the rat race of the busy ministry that he heads up.

3. Shepherding also means that we *protect* them. We need to keep a watchful eye for predators intent on leading them astray.

But David said to Saul, "Your servant has been keeping his father's sheep. When a lion or a bear came and carried off a sheep from the flock, I went after it, struck it and rescued the sheep from its mouth."

(1 Samuel 17:34–35)

Peter warns, "[our] enemy, the devil prowls around like a *roaring lion* looking for someone to devour" (1 Peter 5:8). Quite sobering, isn't it? We cannot afford to let down our guard – ever! Even when (or especially when) we are on holiday. We need to look out for those who are in our care. Are the people who influence their lives those who will draw them deeper into God's presence, or are they friends who will draw them away from God? I need to clarify that it is not wise for us to take on the role of being the Holy Spirit in their lives! However, if I am going to take my role seriously as a mum or dad in the house of God, then I need to do all I can to protect them, just as I would do for my own biological children.

As parents, we have an obligation to our children to keep a watchful eye on what enters through the door of our homes. We are the ones who determine and choose to say "yes, you may enter" or "no, you are not welcome here". As leaders, we need to be aware of who and what is entering our sheep pens. I believe we are called to protect our people in the same way that a shepherd protects his sheep (John 10:12, NIV).

4. Shepherding means that we *bind up the injured*. There are so many wounded and hurting Christians in the church today. I believe it is imperative that we constantly train people in the body of Christ who are able to deal with the deep aches and wounds of the heart. I feel so sad when I think about how many Christians end up carrying the baggage of their past into their future. God never intended for it to be this way. We all have a past. We have all had issues from our childhood or adulthood that we have had to face and learn to put behind us.

When we first moved to England, we lived with a couple in London for eighteen months before moving to Maidstone and, as a result, we see Marcel and Carol as part of our family. Marcel is an incredibly caring man who would not say a harsh word to anyone. Carol, also gentle and kind in nature, had been struggling with a bad dose of flu and was not enjoying the overrated experience of standing under Big Ben at midnight as we entered the new millennium. It was freezing cold, Westminster Bridge was packed way beyond capacity and Carol was feeling very unhappy – and we all knew it. Eventually, Marcel turned to Carol and said, "Just get over it!" What made this scenario so memorable was the fact that it was so out of character for Marcel to react in this way. I believe we reach a point when we too need to say, "Get over it!" There comes a time when, after we have ministered to our ladies, we need to encourage them to make the decision to move on, leaving the past in the past.

The problem is that some people can begin to find their identity in their greatest weaknesses. I know a lady I'll call Angela who struggles with fear and intimidation.

Although Angela has learned the truth of God's Word and understands that "God has not given [her] a spirit of fear, but of power and of love and of a sound mind" (2 Timothy 1:7, NKJV), she continues to be fearful. Why, you might ask? Because it has become a part of who she is. Were she to lay it down, she would need a whole new identity – which can be quite a daunting prospect. Praise God, Angela has walked with a leader who has diligently held her accountable in the way she habitually perceives things and slowly God is beginning to renew her mind. Part of our role as shepherds is to enlighten God's people to the truth that we can live in freedom.

We need to make sure that we are encouraging those with whom we are walking to face up to their past and no longer allow those experiences to dictate their future. According to Paul's second letter to the Corinthians, "Therefore, if anyone is in Christ, he is a new creation; the old has gone, the new has come..." (2 Cor 5:17, NIV).

5. Finally, shepherding means that we *bring back the strays and search for the lost*. In nature, sheep are prone to wander off, which must be a nightmare for the shepherd who is trying to keep track of where all his sheep are. In Bible times, when a lamb consistently wandered off, the shepherd would look for the lost lamb and draw it back to himself using his staff. If the same lamb continued to wander, the shepherd would do something a bit more drastic. You see, the shepherd knows about the dangers that are constantly lurking and that the sheep's lives are at risk. He also knows that a wandering sheep will lead the others astray too. In order to save the life of the wandering lamb, he would break its leg, bind up the wounded leg and then keep the lamb close to himself until the leg had completely healed. Only then would he release the lamb back to the rest of the flock.

Roy Gustafson, who has led many parties to Israel, tells in his book, *In His Hand* about a sheep that was always wandering off and, in the process, leading other sheep astray.

> Membership in the flock carries certain responsibilities, and as much as the shepherd feels a real affection for his animals, discipline is the only thing that will keep them together, as they must be kept together for their well-being and their safety. So to cure this sheep of its self-willed ways, the shepherd had broken its leg, and then hand fed and carried it till the bone was mended, and (hopefully) its waywardness.[1]

I know that "straying people" have caused a huge amount of heartache for church leaders worldwide. The problem isf that it is not only their lives that are affected; straying sheep will inevitably lead the younger lambs astray too! The longer the sheep are left to stray, the further away from the shepherd they will roam. We need to be there at the earliest signs of straying. The longer we leave it, the harder it will be to bring them back. Once they are away from the protection that the body of Christ offers, they become open and vulnerable to the attack of the enemy. This leaves not only the sheep at risk, but the lambs unprepared and vulnerable too. The consequences of such straying for the young are a very real concern, as the lambs will rapidly follow the sheep and end up paying the price. While straying is may be a choice on the part of the grown sheep, the lambs are profoundly influenced by them – this illustrates the influence of older Christians on those who are younger, in both spiritual and physical maturity. This adds a sense of urgency to our efforts to find the lost and straying.

I have witnessed that one of the biggest strategies of the enemy at this stage of straying is deception. Often, although they may know they have drifted, they somehow believe that they are still safe and that they know what they are doing. They think it is OK to indulge just a little in the things of the world; that they've got plenty of time to sort things out later. How wrong they are!

> As it is, you *do not belong* to the world, but I have
> chosen you out of the world.
>
> (John 15:19, NIV)

The magnet of the world is incredibly strong and yet what the world has to offer is so transient. It focuses on meeting our immediate desires with absolutely nothing of eternal value.

> Do not love the world or anything in the world.
> If anyone loves the world, the love of the Father
> is not in him. For everything in the world – the
> cravings of sinful man, the lust of his eyes and
> the boasting of what he has and does – comes
> not from the Father but from the world. The
> world and its desires pass away, but the man
> who does the will of God lives forever .
>
> (1 John 2:15–17 NIV)

The balance in this is that even though we are called to bring back the strays and the lost, something that my husband, Michael, often says is that "we can never be more interested in someone's destiny than they are themselves". My daughter Amy has recently finished writing her end of year exams. She is a very capable student with high aspirations for a great career. As parents, we can encourage her and provide opportunities and an environment that is conducive for her to achieve her full potential. What we cannot do, however, is work and study for her. She is now old enough to take responsibility for the choices that she makes concerning her studies. In the words of the well-known saying, "You can lead a horse to water, but you cannot make it drink!"

Part 2: God's Rod

I was rather surprised to learn that the rod is just as important to a shepherd as his staff. Generally, a rod is made from a carefully chosen, straight young oak tree and is about two feet long. Firstly, the bulb at the beginning of the root (about the size of a man's fist) is trimmed to make the head of a club. Next, a hole is carved through the rod so that it can be tied to the shepherd's belt, or hang from his wrist.

Most of us know that sheep have no natural defences to fight off prey. They don't have claws, horns, tusks, spines, shells, or fangs. The only defence that a sheep has is the shepherd and his rod. Armed with this *protective* device, the shepherd can confidently lead the flock, swinging the rod back and forth to frighten any enemies, thereby preparing the way for the sheep.

Being a friend to someone and walking side by side as we journey through life is an incredible privilege. There are times of fun, laughter and good fellowship but, in the more serious moments, one of the expectations that I have of my friends is that they are always honest with me. I would far sooner hear an honest, possibly more brutal opinion, than have my ears tickled by sweet insincerity. It is so important that we learn to trust one another and not be afraid to ask the hard questions.

I grew up in a home where my brothers and I, and even my mum to a certain extent, tended to steer clear of any form of confrontation. This was because it was more comfortable to keep the peace. Dad was different! He was the undoubted head of our home. He is incredibly loving and kind but also someone who naturally walks in authority. I have always really admired his courage to stand up for what he believes to be right – even at the risk of being misunderstood or rejected.

I remember a situation once when my dad felt he had been unfairly treated. He had needed to pop into town and parked his car where there was some question regarding whether or not it was a legitimate parking place. I am not sure whether the traffic department in George, South Africa, had ever encountered other motorists confused about this whole issue but as there were no signs or lines to communicate otherwise, my dad chose this as his spot. He could not have been in the shop for more than fifteen minutes, and – you've guessed it – returned to his car to find a hefty parking ticket! He was not amused. He marched straight to the traffic department to argue his case. He felt that by parking there he was in no way obstructing or endangering any other vehicles and if the traffic department needed to keep this space clear, then they should communicate their wishes clearly to the public via a painted yellow line. He demanded not only for his fine to be squashed but also for the head of the traffic department to send him a letter of apology for the inconvenience caused and time wasted. He still has that letter from the traffic department to this day!

The thing about my dad is that he is never rude, unkind or disrespectful when he confronts a situation and all the while that I lived at home, I rarely heard him raise his voice. Confrontation is not about bullying or manipulating a situation to get your way; it is about standing up for what you believe to be right.

Michael is also a man with high principles and standards; he is not afraid to confront. When we were first married, the mere thought of confrontation used to leave me with my heart racing, palms sweating and an overwhelming feeling of nausea. I am not sure why I used to be so afraid – but then again, a lot of things seemed to scare me! I suppose my biggest fear was a potential "big" reaction from the person being confronted. It just seemed so much easier to swallow any hurt and sweep tricky situations under the carpet. I was aware that my personality wrestled with the issue of was I "a man or a mouse"! The mouse was mostly what the world saw while the "man in me" usually remained unheard and unseen deep within. Jesus is referred to as both the lion and the lamb. I have yet to come across a more gentle creature than a newborn lamb. But then there is the Lion of Judah and we had better be found ready when He roars! As I have begun to embrace fully all that God has created within me, the gentle lion is awaking from its slumber. Praise God, I have grown and been set free from my fears and insecurities. It has not been a comfortable journey but I realize now that I am spoiled for anything less. This does not mean that I now actually enjoy confrontation, it just means that I am secure enough to stand up for what I believe to be right and can cope with being misunderstood or even rejected.

In leadership, I believe we have a responsibility to ask the ladies with whom we are walking those hard questions. This is not always comfortable. These may include questions such as, "How are you growing in your relationship with God?" or "What do you feel God is saying to you at the moment?" It could perhaps be looking at difficulties in their relationships that may be as a result of unforgiveness, or even questions as to how they manage their time if it happens to be an issue with which they struggle.

Although we don't necessarily enjoy the proverbial 'kick up the butt', deep down we know that it is a part of our maturing process. When looking at the Scriptures, a rod is used in the context of discipline. The writer of Proverbs highlights the importance of discipline in a child's life.

> He who spares the rod hates his son,
> but he who loves him is careful to discipline him.
>
> *(Proverbs 13:24, NIV)*

> Do not withhold discipline from a child;
> if you punish him with the rod, he will not die.
>
> *(Proverbs 23:13, NIV)*

The rod clearly has two different uses. Firstly, when used by a shepherd, we can conclude that it is not only used as a defensive weapon of *protection* but also as an instrument of *discipline*. We are God's children and, as our Father, He disciplines us as He sees fit.

> And you have forgotten that word of encouragement that addresses you as sons: "My son, do not make light of the Lord's discipline, and do not lose heart when he rebukes you, because the Lord disciplines

those he loves, and he punishes everyone he accepts as a son." Endure hardship as discipline; God is treating you as sons. For what son is not disciplined by his father? If you are not disciplined (and everyone undergoes discipline), then you are illegitimate children and not true sons. Moreover, we have all had human fathers who disciplined us and we respected them for it. How much more should we submit to the Father of our spirits and live! Our fathers disciplined us for a little while as they thought best; but God disciplines us for our good, that we may share in his holiness.

(Hebrews 12:5–10, NIV)

We have been looking at the issue regarding our responsibility towards those whom God has placed in our care. I believe that as shepherds and leaders of God's people, we carry both the rod as well as the staff, and one without the other would result in a poorly equipped shepherd, an unbalanced church leader and a very insecure flock! It is so much easier to think of shepherding God's people just with the staff, but the Word is clear that both need to be in operation in order for us to find comfort for our souls.

In 1 Peter 2:25 we read: "For you were like sheep going astray, but now you have returned to the Shepherd and *Overseer* of your souls" (NIV). I love the way the Amplified Bible puts it: "For you were going astray like [so many] sheep, but now you have come back to the Shepherd and *Guardian* (the Bishop) of your souls."

This Scripture refers to Jesus as the One who shepherds and *guards* (watches over) our souls!

Keep watch over yourselves and all the flock of
which the Holy Spirit has made you *overseers*. Be
shepherds of the church of God, which He bought
with His own blood. I know that after I leave, savage
wolves will come in among you and will not spare
the flock.

(Acts 20:28–29, NIV)

The Greek word for "overseer" is *episkopeo* which means
"to look upon, inspect, oversee, look after, care for, to look
carefully, beware". The responsibility we carry in our role
as overseers of the body of Christ is awesome and, for me,
has sometimes been a little overwhelming. Michael and I
were both twenty-four years old when we were first called
into full-time ministry in a church called Harvest in Port
Elizabeth, South Africa. After leading one of the adult
zones in Harvest for just under two years, we were asked
to consider moving to a small town called Queenstown
where, for the first time, we would carry responsibility for
the whole church.

We arrived in Queenstown during a particularly
challenging season within the life of the church. Now aged
only twenty-six, what life experience could we possibly
have in comparison to the many people in the church who
were old enough to be our parents? I needed to hear clearly
from God that it was right for us to have moved there. God
was gracious and spoke to me from the book of Jeremiah,
saying:

"Ah, Sovereign Lord," I said, 'I do not know how
to speak; I am only a child." But the Lord said to
me, "Do not say, 'I am only a child.' You must go to

everyone I send you to and say whatever I command you. Do not be afraid of them, for I am with you and will rescue you," declares the Lord.

(Jeremiah 1:6–8, NIV)

Through this Scripture, God clearly showed me that the right to speak into the life of another has nothing to do with physical age. Instead, it has everything to do with hearing the voice of God and acting on it from a place of wholeness.

This does not necessarily mean that we have automatic access to anyone who crosses our paths! We carry the responsibility to oversee only the lives of very specific people that God has entrusted to our care. In the context of mentoring, this applies to the ladies who have chosen to be part of the year's commitment and who have asked for our input and care. This is where we, as their leaders, are obligated to take up our role to not only shepherd and nurture them but also to be guardians over their souls (Acts 20:28). In other words, if there are any adjustments that need making, we need to – in love – guide them in the right direction.

So what, then, is the balance? Why are we so afraid of confronting people? I think that in general we tend to want to steer clear of confrontation for the sake of maintaining the peace. I used to be absolutely terrified of any form of confrontation and would avoid it at all costs. I used to worry about so many things; I was worried about offending and hurting the person; I was worried about the real possibility of being rejected by them; but most of all, I was worried about an angry response. I firmly agree with Tim Elmore as he writes in his book, *Mentoring*:

I don't believe that any healthy, balanced person actually enjoys confronting someone over a sin, attitude, omission, gossip, or disobedience. Those kinds of meetings always seem to cause our stomachs to churn, our hands and heads to sweat, and our wills to weaken.[2]

A lack of godly confrontation causes strife and insecurities to abound. It is critical that we understand that it is the level of relationship that will determine the extent to which we can confront. I realized, with fear and trepidation, that I had a responsibility towards others and the level of relationship I built would directly impact my effectiveness.

In case there are any doubts in your mind concerning this godly principle, then take some time to meditate on a few Scriptures:

... warn those who are idle, encourage the timid, help the weak, be patient with everyone..

(1 Thessalonians 5:14, NIV)

... Scripture is... profitable for teaching, for reproof, for correction, for training...

(2 Timothy 3:16, NASB)

preach... reprove, rebuke, exhort...

(2 Timothy 4:2–4, NASB)

... warning and admonishing [warn by reminding] everyone...

(Colossians 1:28, AMPLIFIED BIBLE)

I love this quotation by Alfred Whitehead: "Apart from blunt truth, our lives sink decadently amid the perfume of hints and suggestions!"[3]

What is our ultimate aim when bringing correction to someone? It should *always* be to see them transformed by the power of God. Not condemnation but transformation. As we meet with the ladies, we need to remember a few important principles:

1. It is important to make sure we have thought about a suitable venue for a meeting of this nature. It is pretty obvious that coffee shops and restaurants are not ideal. I would suggest that our homes are probably better because we have more opportunity to be able to set the tone of the meeting and can minimize any possible interruptions. Admonishing requires a private and safe place.

2. It is so important to remember that our standard in everything *must*, without a doubt, be the Word of God. We need to be completely clear about this before the meeting even starts so that we are able to take a stand. Confronting someone who is very talkative can be challenging if we do not keep a clear head. We must deal primarily with principles from the Word of God – and *not* be led by our emotions.

3. We must learn to resist the temptation of reasoning from our personal preferences with people. When dealing with someone of a different culture, it is important to have a thorough understanding of them within the context of their culture. Often, what is acceptable in one culture is frowned upon in another culture and we need to be aware of these differences. Again, this is why it

is so important that our standard *must* be the Word of God, rather than personal preference.

4. To not mention our attitude at this point would be foolish. We need to make sure that the person we are dealing with knows beyond a shadow of a doubt that our love for them is never in question. The same is also true in disciplining our own children – because they know how much we love them. Research has shown that disciplined children feel much safer and more secure than children who grow up without boundaries. It is important to be aware of the fact that the attitude we display will often speak louder than the actual words we are saying. Remember that truth without grace can have extremely negative repercussions.

5. It is important for us as leaders to initiate the process. It could be that the person involved is not even aware that a situation has developed. It would therefore be disastrous to sit around waiting for the offending person to make contact with us. We have a clear policy regarding this in Jubilee Church – *nip it in the bud*! The longer we wait, the more the situation tends to grow, affecting more and more people.

6. Once the meeting is underway, we have discovered that the best way to raise an issue is to first affirm the person; acknowledging growth and strengths you have seen in their lives. We can then gently begin to point out the area that we are concerned about, always showing them a way out. It is important to be thoroughly prepared for a meeting of this nature. We must make sure that we are ready with suggestions regarding the way forward and let them know that we would be letting them down

if we did not take our role seriously and did not follow through and hold them accountable in this area.

7. Always end the meeting on a positive note. We must let them know how much we love them and that we believe in them. We all make mistakes and a common saying that we have as leaders in Jubilee Church is, "Have a mistake on me!" It is possible they have not yet been equipped in this area, making this an ideal opportunity for learning. Remember, you can never correct until you have equipped!

I have been surprised by the number of ladies who have responded to correction with, "Thank you for being so honest with me; nobody has ever told me that before. I did not realize I responded in that way." I would like to share one such testimony of a girl who embraced Jesus not only as her saviour but also allowed Him to become Lord of her life. I will call the girl Elizabeth. When we first met her, she was in a place of brokenness and despair. She began a journey to restoration and wholeness that was slow and, at times, difficult. We were about to launch our second year of mentoring and, for Elizabeth, this seemed to hold the key to the breakthrough she so longed for. She approached Hazel and asked her whether she could be a part of the mentoring. This was a difficult situation to handle, because although our hearts were to see her restored, we felt that the timing was not yet right as she would struggle with the monthly meetings. When the mentoring groups meet together each month, the ladies are encouraged to open up and share freely as to what God is doing in their lives. We felt that this may overwhelm Elizabeth and that should she experience a real low, her emotions and personal turmoil could possibly dominate and thus influence the whole group. As leaders, it is important to consider not only the individual but also the impact a person could have on a group as a whole.

In love, Hazel explained why we felt that she was not yet ready to embark on such a process. Although her initial response was one of hurt and disappointment, while praying about it, she came to terms with our decision. She spoke to Hazel and asked whether she would be able to read all the books and complete an assignment each month, even though she would not officially be part of a group. She would also meet regularly and be accountable to Hazel.

Elizabeth was so faithful in walking this road. She read every book diligently and poured out her heart as she completed each assignment. She was beginning to take bigger steps forward. By the end of the year, we felt that she was ready to be a part of a group situation and so we sent her a letter of invitation to come on board for the following year of mentoring. I have her letter of response with me and I would like to share it with you.

Hazel,

Thank you for giving me the opportunity to be part of the mentoring course. I would love to do the mentoring this year!

I feel that being an unofficial member this last year has been a result of God preparing me for taking a more involved role this year.

I think that God will use this course to develop maturity – both spiritually and personally.

I will learn to pray with a partner, which will be challenging, but essential.

I will learn to discuss my feelings and worries with other people – through which I'll become more open to sharing within a group environment.

It will help me to build new friendships and to get to know people better.

I think this will be a really great experience for me. I believe God will use this course to do lots in my life.

I'm really excited to be involved and am really looking forward to this next year.

Thank you!

Elizabeth started a part-time job during her year of mentoring and, a few months later, she married the man of her dreams. I stand amazed at God's faithfulness in the lives of individuals who are ready to embrace God's heart; a heart which not only shepherds His flock, but also guards over their souls, ensuring godly boundaries remain in place.

I am so grateful for the safety and comfort that I have found as I have learned to trust others and allow godly men and women to speak into my life. I know that because they love me, they will always be honest with me.

NOTES

1 Roy Gustafson, *In His Hand*

2 Tim Elmore, *Mentoring*, Indianapolis, Indiana: Wesleyan Publishing House, 1995.

3 Quoted in Tim Elmore, Mentoring.

A Final Thought

Heather writes...

My maternal grandfather was one of the most wonderful men that I have ever met and, although he was South African by birth, he was definitely very British in nature. His full name was Cecil Egerton Wingfield Douglass but we fondly knew him as Gee. Every week, my brothers Bruce and John and I were completely enthralled as our mum used to read us his long, handwritten letters. These letters detailed the most entertaining stories, where our pets played the main characters. At the end of each school term, the envelope that arrived was always a bit thicker than usual, as it was sure to contain ten South African rand for each of us to go and "smell the roses". This meant that the next trip into town with my mother would have to include a stop for milkshakes. I clearly remember the big shopping expeditions we enjoyed with Granny and Gee when they came to stay with us each year. My gran's role was to make sure my brothers and I were properly behaved, while Gee's priority by mid-morning was to stop and smell the roses! What a highlight... finding a lovely tea room and finally being able to sit down to enjoy the finer things in life such as tea served in a proper tea cup, with a pancake of our choice. The other not-so-fortunate shoppers were left alone to battle their way through the hustle and bustle that comes with shopping – while we were living life big!

What did Jesus mean when He said, "The thief comes

only to steal, kill and destroy; I came that they may have life, and have it abundantly" (John 10:10, NASB)? He did *not* say, "I have come that you may have good meetings, or that you may have a clean house!" The Greek word used for "abundantly" is *perissos* which means superior, extraordinary, more remarkable, or more excellent. This is what we mean when we say *live life big*. This will probably have many different meanings for us as women but, besides my family, a part of my abundant life is to be able to make a difference; to know and live in God's purpose for my life. It is so important, however, to always determine in our hearts to keep our lives balanced. I know of many people out there serving God with their whole hearts at the expense of spending quality time with their own families. Living life big includes finding that balance.

I can see only a portion of the road that God has called me to walk, stretching out ahead – parts of this road appear straightforward, an easy stroll, while other parts have great big boulders that will potentially block my way. There have been times when I have been able to see the boulders from afar but there have also been times that were if not for a friend showing me the way, I would have blindly stumbled and possibly even fallen. Whatever part of the journey I am on, just knowing that I have friends and family walking beside me makes my journey so much easier. Sometimes, God requires me to deal with the boulders in my life on my own and in these times, as I look to the side of the road, I draw great comfort from the friends that I see cheering me on. I must admit, there have been times in my life when I have not even had the energy to want to look at the boulder; when I have needed a boot up my butt! Then there have also been times when friends, with incredible insight and wisdom, have come alongside me and gently helped me to climb over the boulders. I am not sure how well I would do in life without the friends that God has graciously brought across my path. He knows exactly what we need to make it in life.

> And my God will meet all your needs according to his glorious riches in Christ Jesus.
>
> *(Philippians 4:19, NIV)*

Hazel and I are cheering you on; we may not necessarily know you but we carry you in our hearts. Look to the side of your road and hear us as we shout, "You can do it!" We know you can – because He did it for us. And if He could rescue us, then He can definitely give you the courage and grace to rise up into the fullness of all that He has called you to be.

Hazel writes...

Recently, I watched a film called *The Yes Man*. It was the story of a man who had been dealt a few tough blows in life and consequently said "no" to everything. He had stepped out of life and was operating in a dull form of existence. One day, he had a strange encounter which resulted in him having to say "yes" to everything. As he was forced to use this new and unfamiliar word, "yes", a whole world opened up to him. He got promoted at work. He had fun with friends. He met a girl and he fell in love. His life was changed for ever. He started living his life. It was a funny, entertaining film but I found the storyline inspiring. How often do we say "no" without even thinking about it? How often, on a more personal level, have I said "no" because I was too afraid to take a risk?

I have stayed in bed for far too long, hiding under

the duvet and shrinking back from the world. I have too often gone down the path of least resistance and settled for second best. I am faced with a choice, to live life big, or to just stay in bed. Some days are easier than others. There are times when everything within me wants to be comfortable, where stepping out and facing the day takes courage, grit and determination. But now, staying in bed has lost its attraction. I am too restless for *more* to lie back and vegetate a moment longer. The duvet has been ditched and I am getting dressed. I don't know what today will hold, what challenges I will face, or what life will throw at me but the curtains are open, the sun is shining and today I choose to "live life big".

Everyone is on a journey; everyone has as story to tell. As Heather and I have walked together, we have gained a clearer picture of what our journey is all about and where it is taking us. But we are not the only two on this road. You are walking beside us. We trust and pray that you too will discover and realize the potential that you carry and that together we can all see our potential released for the furthering of God's kingdom.

There is a whole life waiting to be lived and we urge you – do not stay in bed! It could be fatal; bedsores are just the beginning of the end. Come on – live life big!

Appendix

Practical Aspects of Mentoring: Hints and Tips

by Hazel and Heather

Hazel writes...

One of the things that Heather and I love about mentoring is that it is not just a programme-based structure but a lifestyle. However, a good framework is essential and in this chapter we want to share with you some of the practical tools that we have found useful and effective.

Each mentoring group consists of a number of ladies with a leader and a co-leader. We initially had ten ladies in each group in addition to the two leaders but found that meeting one to one with each lady during the course of a month proved challenging, especially for those of us with busy schedules. We now try to have no more than eight ladies in each group, including the two leaders. When we ask a lady to join the mentoring programme, it is by invitation only and we send her a personal letter asking her to prayerfully consider joining us for the year. Although it is our heart that every woman in Jubilee Church has an opportunity to do the mentoring, there are a few things that need to be considered. Is she leaning forward in the Spirit and is she teachable? Is she in a place where she can realistically commit to the programme and will she work well in a group environment? We ask her to consider the following requirements before replying to us in writing:

1. To attend the Mentoring Launch Day at the beginning of the year where the heart of mentoring is imparted.

2. To meet once a month as a group at the leader's home, for a time of encouragement, impartation and fellowship.

3. To meet once a week with a prayer partner, to be faithful in praying together and building friendships.

4. To read a designated book or portion of Scripture, or both, each month and to journal as they read.

5. To complete an assignment that needs to be handed in at each monthly meeting.

6. To meet once a month with their mentor for input and accountability.

7. To attend the end of year mentoring banquet to celebrate God's goodness during the year.

Let's look in detail at each of the components of the mentoring programme and how they work.

The Mentoring Launch Day

We usually start the year with a launch day, where all the ladies from the different groups can meet together. One of the primary aims of this day is for Heather and I to impart our heart and the vision that God has given to us for the mentoring.

We like to start the day with something fun and light-hearted that will put the ladies at ease and break down any awkward barriers. It is natural for us to feel apprehensive when we first go along to something new and unknown, so it is important that the ladies feel reassured that they are in a safe environment.

We have a special time of praise and worship, where we can come into God's presence and have an opportunity to lay aside anything that may hinder us from getting the best out of the year. This gives the ladies time to prepare themselves both mentally and spiritually for all that God has in store for them.

They are introduced to their group leaders, meet the other ladies in their groups and are put with their prayer partners. We ask them to consider their expectations for the year and think about what they are hoping to get out of the mentoring process. They fill in a questionnaire that gives us, as leaders, useful and relevant information that we can build upon over the course of the year (see the Resources chapter). This lays a good foundation for what lies ahead and helps to set the standard right at the onset.

Heather writes...

The Monthly Meeting

This is one of the most exciting and relevant parts of mentoring. It is a time when the whole group meets together to enjoy fellowship and friendship and also to minister and encourage one another. It is a place where we can be real and feel safe and secure; a place where we know that we are loved and cherished; where we "do life" together!

We usually launch mentoring at the start of the academic year. It is at this time that we give the ladies all the dates for the monthly meetings that are to take place for the whole year. We encourage the ladies to diarize these dates and to make attendance a priority. It is so frustrating for the leaders to have women not able to attend, as it is hard to play catch-up with regards to the focus and direction of what God is saying to them for the next month. Another reason we take this commitment so seriously is because there have been many times when we have prepared activities for the ladies to do with their prayer partners and, if one person is not there, it can be rather difficult. Because we send the ladies a letter of invitation that clearly outlines their commitment for the year, there are times when we need to remind the ladies of the importance of seeing a commitment through, rather than being defeated when obstacles arise. It is important to note that there is a fine line between being legalistic in these areas and walking through the principle of commitment.

Planning the Monthly Meeting

Our senior leadership team usually meets together about midway through the month to pray and prepare for the next monthly meeting. We then meet with the mentoring leaders at least a week before the next meeting to give them a skeleton copy of the evening.

We never go into a leader's planning meeting unsure of where God is leading us for the next month. There was a time when we really wrestled with the fact that we wanted the leaders to be able to take "ownership" of the meetings they were running; that we were not simply dictating to them what they should do. We realized that it was more productive and effective when there were just two or three heads hearing from God and overseeing the general direction of the mentoring year, rather than a whole group of leaders. The leaders could then take ownership through their individual input to the already prepared framework.

1. Before the Meeting

Venue

We always encourage our leaders to host their meetings in either of their homes, rather than in a church building or in the house of one of the ladies in their group. There are a couple of reasons for this. Firstly, we are trying to create a sense of family and belonging and a church hall or building does not easily facilitate this in a small-group environment. In terms of restricting the venue to either of the leaders' homes – we are able to have more influence in creating the right vibe or atmosphere. I know that there was a time when Hazel felt that she would like to give all the ladies a chance to be able to host the meetings. But once, when Hazel and her co-leader arrived at the lady's home expecting an atmosphere of peace and tranquillity, you can imagine her dismay at finding complete chaos! The poor woman whose house it was had been running late all day. She was still trying to clear the dinner dishes away! This resulted in both the leaders doing all they could to help get everything ready for the meeting. We encourage our leaders to meet together half an hour before the meeting is due to start so that they can spend time praying. This is usually a precious time together where we lay aside any burdens and stress from the day as we get into God's presence to seek His face for the meeting that lies ahead.

It is probably worth mentioning here that the spiritual battle can become quite intense during the time leading up to the meeting. Prayer and standing together is a vital part of our personal preparation.

Creating an Atmosphere

- Candles/good lighting always creates an intimate atmosphere for those arriving. They can immediately feel at peace and sense God's presence.

- It is lovely to have background music playing, especially at the beginning of the year when the ladies do not know each other that well. There is nothing worse than moments of awkward silence.

- We should make sure that tea/coffee is set out and prepared before the meeting so that we are available to welcome the ladies. During my early days of leading meetings, there were a couple of times where I ended up running around like a headless chicken, still filling the kettle as people were arriving and regretting the fact that I had not remembered to turn the dishwasher on!

- It is important to make sure that the room being used is clean and tidy. I struggle to connect with God while sitting on squeaky toys, amid the clutter of books and papers which have been left lying around.

- When leaders have young children, it is vital that they plan their day so that they are able to spend quality time with their children before the meeting begins. If this is not possible, they need to communicate to their children when they have next planned some quality time together. Pressing needs, such as completing homework for the next day, need to be taken into consideration. Is their father perhaps able to help out or could it have been done the previous day? Because children can be so unpredictable, getting them fed, watered and ready for bed is often stressful at the best of times. An old trick of the enemy is to try to steal God's peace and His joy from us whilst we are preparing for the meeting. We must guard our hearts at this time. Do not allow the enemy access!

• If we are married, it is also important that we guard our relationship with our husbands during this time of preparation. It is very hard to have a "happy face" with a "How can I help you?" attitude through gritted teeth as we make a mental note of what we should have said during a heated debate with our husbands moments before the meeting is due to begin!

It has been amusing to discover as we compared notes that usually, without fail, the first Wednesday of each month (mentoring night) has been one where we have needed to face unexpected turmoil.

We often wrongly assume that some of the scenarios described above would not need to be mentioned but one thing I have learned... take *nothing* for granted! Our leaders need to be well trained and equipped in every area so that these mistakes can be avoided.

Part of the reason why our ladies enjoy the monthly meetings so much is because they are unpredictable. As there is a real danger of falling into a rut when it comes to planning meetings, it is important to vary the structure and order of the evening.

2. The Welcome

Please make sure you have your "friendly" face on! What I mean by this is that it is important to leave any issues we are walking through at the foot of the cross before the meeting starts. We need to remember that *we* are the ones who set the tone for the meeting. If we are feeling downhearted, we can be sure that the group will pick up on it! This does not mean that we need to pretend about where we are at but as a leader, we need wisdom when being real. If I am going through a particularly hard time, I will cautiously let the group know, but will not in any way allow it to influence the direction in which the meeting is heading.

Hazel once hung a black bin liner on her door and, as the ladies arrived, she encouraged them to symbolically dump their baggage from the day into the bin liner. This caused plenty of laughter and the meeting got off to a good start.

- Ladies generally respond well to being hugged. I realize that some women may feel a bit awkward in this area but there have been occasions where ladies have been ministered to purely through a genuine, heartfelt hug.

- It is important to relax and be yourself. Do not put pressure on yourself to perform as you try to keep the conversation flowing. This is exhausting! Allow things to flow as naturally as possible.

- Be aware of those ladies with quieter personalities. Find ways to draw them into the conversation. On the same note, there always seems to be someone in every group who can be loud and domineering; you may need a quiet word with them at some point if they are not aware of this.

3. Tea and Coffee

Good fellowship usually occurs over a cup of tea and possibly something to eat. It is a vital part of the meeting and should not be rushed for the sake of time. We usually allow at least twenty minutes for this.

This part of the evening does not necessarily need to be scheduled at the beginning. Having it right at the end is sometimes a good way to close a meeting. The only downside to this, however, is that some ladies may need to rush off and will thus miss out on the opportunity to just "hang out". Having tea and coffee in the middle of an evening is sometimes a nice break, a time when people can stretch their legs and maybe even go to the loo!

Instead of tea and coffee, we have had hot chocolate with cream and marshmallows in winter. One evening, we gave the ladies soup. Summer is a great time to make fruit smoothies or ice cream sundaes and enjoy them in the garden.

4. Ice Breakers

Fun Ice Breakers

I believe that one of the reasons our church is growing so rapidly is because of the genuine love and care that we have for one another. We have become one large family and we endeavour in all of our meetings to have a bit of family time where we can laugh and play together.

I am aware that for some, the very thought of an ice breaker seems threatening. But we have seen that this is actually a vital tool in breaking down barriers. It is important to make sure when planning an ice breaker that the age and dynamics of the group have been taken into consideration. The younger the group, the more energetic and physically challenging an ice breaker can be.

My husband, Michael, wrote the book *Red Hot Ice Breakers* which contains over three hundred different ideas to help get any meeting going. These range from those that are wild and wacky to the more serious, deep discussion starters. He now has a second book full of ideas for ice breakers called *300+ Sizzling Ice Breakers*.

We have certainly done some crazy things in our meetings, with the sole purpose of "breaking the ice". We have made up impromptu dramas; we have sung songs; gone on treasure hunts; competed to be the winning group in quizzes; and played many silly games. One that stands out (which is surprisingly appropriate for any age group) is to tape a one-metre piece of string to the end of one's nose, with a marshmallow tied to the other end. Everyone then stands in a circle seeing who can be the first one to successfully fling the marshmallow into their mouths with their hands kept behind their backs! When we did this, amid much hilarity, the ladies finished up feeling relaxed and energized by one another; their burdens seeming slightly less daunting.

Serious Ice Breakers

Ice breakers can also take on a more serious tone where we can get to know one another on a deeper level. This can be in the form of a question; for example, you may ask: "Who was the most influential person in your life between the ages of five and twelve?" This gives each member of the group an opportunity to share a snippet of their upbringing, which automatically takes the relationships to a deeper level. We have been surprised by how often this particular question has led to ministry later on in the meeting.

It is important, although not always appropriate, that the ladies have an opportunity to *briefly* share where they are in life. A good ice breaker for this is to give each of the ladies a blank sheet of A4 paper. Then, ask the ladies to illustrate where they are at, using their piece of paper. We have had some ladies tearing their sheets into shreds, while others have made beautiful flowers. Each lady then gets a turn to describe their illustration, which can be followed by a short time of prayer.

I always let the ladies know how much time has been allocated to ensure that our long-winded friends do not take up half the evening! The purpose here is just to touch base rather than to have a summary of their day-to-day activities over the last month. At the start of a new mentoring year, we usually plan for slightly longer times of sharing as this contributes to a deeper bonding within the group.

Another way of sharing is to spend time talking about the book which we have been reading as a group. It was during our very first monthly meeting that I learned a valuable lesson in *how* to facilitate this discussion. What I realized was that each lady will have her own view and personal opinion of each different book and we need to be wise as we consider who the right person is to lead the feedback. The first lady to share at one particular meeting had struggled to get into the book we had just read and was thus quite negative in the way that she shared. It was amazing to see how the whole group was influenced by her negative response, even though I knew for a fact that some of the women had really enjoyed the book.

There were two lessons that I learned that night. If you are trusting for your ladies to share on a deep level, then it is a good idea for one of the leaders to share first, because as they open up and, in a sense, make themselves vulnerable, so the rest of the group will feel safe to follow suit.

The second lesson I learned was the importance of phrasing the question carefully. Whether we enjoy a particular book or not is not really relevant to the rest of the group. What is important, however, is *what God is saying to us through the book* and this is what I usually ask. The book does not necessarily have to suit one's preferred style of writing for God to speak!

5. Worship and Ministry

This is a vital part of the monthly meeting. We used to be of the opinion that in order to enjoy a special time of worship we needed a good musician in the meeting, but soon realized that to have one is usually the exception rather than the norm. Worshipping with a CD playing can be quite meaningful. However, it is important to remember that when using a CD, it is vital that the leader is well prepared and sensitive to the Holy Spirit.

Having a musician is obviously really helpful but certainly not essential and there are many creative ways in which ladies can worship together. For example, worship can be a time of thanksgiving and declaring the goodness of God. Once, with a worship CD playing in the background, we all wrote our own psalms to God and then later, those who felt confident read these to the rest of the group. It was an incredibly special time of worship.

I have known of other groups where the leader has provided paint and paper and, with soft worship music playing, the ladies have painted what they believed God was saying to them, as a form of worship. The non-artistic ladies were initially quite daunted by the thought of "having to produce something" but later reported on how God really ministered to them during this special time.

It is important to have thought about *when* worship would be most appropriate. We tend to worship either just before the impartation time, so that the ladies have had time to prepare their hearts to receive the Word of God, or usually just afterwards. This could easily and naturally lead into a time of ministry, as while some of the ladies are worshipping, others could be praying and ministering to one another.

A time of ministry could take various forms and is very much dependent on how the Spirit is leading. We have had times in our groups when we have prayed for and ministered to each lady individually, trusting God for prophetic words of encouragement. There have been other times when the ladies have paired up in the prayer partners and have maybe shared communion together. They have also shared the servant love of Jesus and washed one another's feet.

I remember one monthly meeting where the leaders made a laminated bookmark for each of the ladies, beautifully designed with the spiritual meaning of each of their names. Each lady was then prayed for and ministered to accordingly. They really appreciated this and I know that they felt incredibly loved and special. What amazes me is how often the meaning of our names reflect an aspect of our personality.

At another meeting, we gave each lady an A4 sheet of paper and asked them to write their names at the top of the page. They then passed their piece of paper to the person on their right who proceeded to write down something positive and encouraging about her. The paper was passed around the whole group for each person to write just one or two lines. The purpose of this activity was for the ladies to realize how much they were valued and loved by their group. I know of many ladies who still to this day carry their A4 papers around with them in their Bibles and on days where they feel defeated, they refer back to it and are once again encouraged.

6. Impartation Time

This is where the heart of where we are going for the next month is shared. The assignment that the ladies are given at the end of the meeting has usually been planned around that which was imparted during this special time.

Again, this can take on a variety of forms. We always encourage our leaders not to see this as a teaching time but as an opportunity to facilitate a group discussion. This is best achieved through careful planning of appropriate questions where we have an opportunity to glean nuggets of truth from one another. It is so important during this time that the leaders consciously draw out the quieter members of the group, giving each person a chance for input. At the same time, it is important to not allow certain ladies to dominate the discussion.

We have had themes such as servanthood; giving; dying to self; obedience. Where appropriate, we have also given the leaders further reading on the given topic in order to help them in their preparation.

The impartation does not, however, necessarily need to take on the form of teaching or facilitating a discussion. It is important that the ladies are taught, practically, how to study the Word and we have used the impartation time for this purpose. You can consider pairing the ladies into their prayer partners and sending them into different parts of the house armed with computers, Greek/Hebrew dictionaries, concordances and commentaries. Together, they can study a specific part of Scripture and then report back to the group what God has shown them. God speaks to us all so differently and the combined wealth of what He says can be amazing!

7. Concluding the Meeting

I have been in many meetings where the ending has not been properly thought through. It is so important to finish the meeting well; to make sure that the ladies are in a good place and that they are not leaving with any unanswered questions.

- It is at this time that the assignment for the following month is discussed so that the ladies are clear about exactly what is expected of them.

- It is also a good time to have a quick look at diaries and to set aside time when you can meet with your ladies for one-to-one meetings.

- Announcements are given, discussing any social events that the group has planned together. This could be anything from a weekend away, a day trip, a movie and popcorn evening, or an afternoon cream tea. It has proved beneficial for the group to spend time together outside of the mentoring meetings.

In one of our mentoring groups, we had a lady who needed to be home by a specific time, so for fear of running late, the leaders did this part of the meeting right at the beginning during their tea and coffee time.

8. After the Meeting

We always encourage our leaders to briefly meet together after the meeting. It is important to discuss the evening in terms of what worked well and what areas could be improved on.

We have found this to be extremely beneficial for numerous reasons. There was once a meeting that I led while Michael was away ministering. The meeting had ended quite late and, because I had a babysitter at home with the girls, I was in a hurry to get back home to them. Although the meeting had been a fairly good one, there were one or two moments that I thought may have worked better by taking a different approach. That night, as I struggled to sleep, I had many hours at my disposal to analyze and reanalyze the meeting. By the time I got up the next morning, the meeting had gone from being OK to absolutely rotten, as I believed the destructive lies of the enemy. By mid-morning the following day, I was ready to give up on being a leader altogether, until I spoke to my co-leader on the phone. Praise God, she was able to give me some much-needed perspective and insight. I was horrified at how quickly the enemy had managed to not only steal my joy, but my confidence too! We need not give the enemy any ground at all to work in our minds, which is why we need to talk through the meeting with our co-leader before going to bed. It is a time where we can give honest and helpful feedback. This is one of the ways that we, as leaders, can embrace an opportunity to really grow in our leadership skills. Receiving what may be defined as "criticism" is not always easy but, because we encourage it to be given in love, it is seen by our leaders as a safe place to grow.

The monthly meeting is thus a time when all the groups simultaneously take the next step in what they feel God is saying to them as a whole. It is a time of fun, laughter, relationship building, ministry and hopefully an impartation of God's Word and His truth into their lives.

Hazel writes...

The Prayer Partners

The prayer partner commitment is a vital part of the mentoring, and enables the ladies to develop and pursue friendships over the course of the year. The two leaders of the group meet together weekly to pray for one another and for the women in their group. They spend time praying at the beginning of the year to decide how best to pair up their ladies. We put the ladies with their prayer partners rather than letting them choose who they want to be with, for a number of reasons. When putting a couple together, we need to consider the dynamic that they will bring. Although we all have a responsibility to pursue, it is true to say that there are those who naturally do this and those who don't. We always try to put a pursuer in each prayer partner relationship, to ensure that they get together regularly and build a good level of friendship. Although it is both the ladies' responsibility to make the thing work, having a natural pursuer in the mix helps to speed up the process.

You will need to consider practical things such as jobs, transport and flexibility when you pair up your ladies, to ensure that they can actually find a time and a place each week to get together! The women really need to make every effort to meet together weekly and to realize that in failing to do so, they not only let themselves down but also their prayer partner. There are times when it is impossible to physically get together, but even then, encourage the ladies to be in regular contact by phone and to still be praying for one another... praying together over the phone can be very effective.

It is important to emphasize to the ladies that the purpose in their getting together is to support one another and not to burden one another! Encourage them to be positive and excited about their prayer partner and to go out of their way to be nothing less than a blessing. This in itself may be a big step up for some women. However, it is critical, right from the start, to encourage them to step out of their comfort zones. You need to explain that this is an opportunity for them not just to get together with already existing friends – it is a chance to build new friendships based on godly principles, laying aside personal agendas and serving one another. We usually ask them to seek God for a word for their prayer partner during the first month and to maybe break bread together. They need to be encouraged to be praying together and not just chatting! Let's face it, we can all be guilty of this. It is a misconception to think that you need to know each other well before you can pray together. In fact, it is as we draw into God's presence together that we are able to let barriers down and be open and honest with one another. Praying together actually speeds up the friendship process. It is the enemy who would have us believe that we cannot pray because we do not know each other well enough.

You will need to explain to your ladies that they are not meeting together to mentor one another or bring counsel and advice. This input will come from their mentors. The purpose of their times together is friendship, encouragement and support… something we all need and benefit from.

We do not always leave the ladies with the same prayer partner throughout the course of the year; sometimes we have changed them halfway through. This is at your discretion and depends very much on how things are going. If a particular couple have not managed to gel or work well together, it may be necessary to change prayer partners. We have found that doing this with the whole group rather than just one couple prevents anyone from feeling that they have failed or let the others down. It can be presented in a very positive way and the rest of the group do not even need to know that there have been issues or difficulties. Wherever possible, our heart is to cover and protect our ladies and not to expose them or make them feel uncomfortable. Therefore, any difficulties need to be handled lovingly and sensitively.

Meeting together with their prayer partners has really helped the ladies in the area of self-discipline, especially in their personal and corporate prayer life. So often we know we should be praying more regularly but struggle to practically build it into our busy schedules. Making a commitment to meet weekly to pray helps to bring a new level of accountability and, even after the year, many ladies still meet and pray together. Some women who have previously found it difficult to even pray out loud have grown in confidence and feel more equipped to pray corporately as well as with their prayer partners.

It has been wonderful to watch and hear testimonies of how friendships have grown and developed over the year, often with the most unexpected pairs. So often there is a cry in their hearts for a deeper level of friendship and the prayer partner relationships have really helped to facilitate this by providing a new level of trust.

The Books and the Word

The Word of God is food for our souls and a light to our feet, yet so many of us fail to read, meditate or even have a sound knowledge of it. Our desire is to raise up daughters who carry a hunger and passion for His Word and who have been equipped to apply what it says to their lives. Nothing is a substitute for the Word of God and although we cover numerous books throughout the course of the year, they are not to replace one's daily reading of the Word of God. This commitment is over and above the members' usual daily quiet times and reading of the Word. Some months we ask the ladies to just read Scripture, sometimes we ask them to read a book and some months we ask for both! It is important to get a healthy balance here and to be careful not to overload the ladies to a point where they can't absorb anything because they are just trying to keep up with the pressure of finishing their book each month. Some books are "meatier" than others and would be better enjoyed over two or even three months, while others are a quick read and can easily be completed within the month.

When we first started mentoring, we thought we would do the same books each year but this idea was quickly abandoned as God showed us that He is a God of the new and the fresh! It seems that books too have seasons and what could be brilliant for one year could be totally wrong for another. As we look back over each year, we can see how God has woven a theme that has come out through the books that we have read. We do not plan all of the books at the beginning of each year but rather seek God for a theme. We try to listen to what the Spirit is saying and be as flexible as possible. As leaders, it is essential that you have read the book before recommending it to your ladies. We are never merely looking for "a good book" but rather for what the Spirit is saying and whether a particular book carries the right message for where the ladies are at. It is important to keep the books as varied as possible and not to get stuck in a rut. We try to have a mixture of books that deal with things on a personal level that the ladies can relate to and identify with. It is also important to guard against the books becoming too inward-looking. Although we are committed to the individual and seeing them come to a place of wholeness, it is good to keep a healthy perspective and help the ladies see that God has more than just them on His mind! Reading a good outward-looking book helps them see beyond themselves and expands their world view. We have read books that equip us, historical books, novels and biographies, all of which have been excellent in their season. Once the next book has been chosen, we order it from our local Christian bookshop in plenty of time for the next monthly meeting.

Often the ladies say that they are very grateful to have a structure to help them read on a regular basis. It is such a good resource for them to build up over the course of the year – books that they can refer back to at any time. They are told at the beginning of the year that they will need to buy their own books each month and encouraged to see this as an investment rather than as an unnecessary expense. Where finances are an issue, it may be good to ask someone else to bless them by helping with the cost each month. We never want anyone to feel unable to do the mentoring due to a lack of finance – and there are many creative ways to cover this so that no one feels disqualified.

Some months we ask the ladies to do a word study on a particular book of the Bible, to vary the versions that they read (for example, NIV, NASB, NKJ and so on) and go more in-depth than they would normally. Meditation and memorizing portions of Scripture are also good practical suggestions that again provide them with tools that they keep long after the year has finished. To be able to quote the Word of God in the face of our enemy in those times when the battle is raging is a good weapon to have in our hand!

The Monthly Assignments

Alongside the monthly book or portion of Scripture, we ask the ladies to complete an assignment. It is important to stress here that this is not merely an academic or an intellectual exercise. Asking the ladies to write down answers to specific questions is helpful for a number of reasons. Firstly, it helps them think through and apply what they have read during the month. How often have you read a great book, only to find that you cannot remember what it was about when you try to recall it a few months later? Asking questions and thinking things through as we read helps us to remember and absorb what we are reading, as well as making sense of it and seeing how it applies on a personal level. The questions are designed to get the ladies to open up and share about the areas that God is putting His finger on.

Another purpose of the assignment is to provide the mentoring leader with a clear sense of where their ladies are at and what issues, if any, need attention. Sometimes, to be asked, "So, where are you at?" is a tough question to answer. But if the mentor has the assignment there in front of them and they have had a good chance to prepare beforehand, they know exactly where the meeting needs to go and what things need to be covered. The questions need to be specific in order to do this successfully, which is why you need to think through them carefully and consider what you want to address. Give your members questions that cannot be answered by a quick 'yes' or 'no'. Ensure that you word them in such a way as to get the most out of your ladies in the context of transparency and openness.

You need to reassure your ladies that the assignments are confidential and that what they share will be kept in total confidence wherever possible. However, there may be some exceptions where you cannot keep what has been shared in confidence. For example, if someone's safety is at risk you will need to tread wisely and cautiously and explain clearly why you need to share what has been written. Remember that in the same way your ladies are choosing to walk in accountability, you too are accountable to your spiritual covering and leadership.

There is often fear or even panic with some ladies when we mention the word "assignment". Breaking the wrong mindset here is essential if you are going to get them to open up and share their feelings with you. You are not interested in the standard of their writing, how good their grammar or spelling is, or how well they have mastered the use of the English language! You are not looking for quantity but quality in what they share. There is nothing worse than having to read through pages of academic waffle only to find that there is no substance to it. On the other end of the scale, though, one-sentence answers often don't provide enough to work with! There is a balance that you need to help them find in order for them to really benefit from the exercise.

We ask our ladies to hand in their assignments at the monthly meeting; they can either be handed in physically or emailed to the leader, who can then print them out and keep them ready for binding. At the end of the year, we hand back all the assignments that the ladies have written, bound and put in folders for them to keep. This usually takes place at the end of year banquet and the ladies have told us how much they appreciate having their work returned. It is a good reminder of the journey they have taken over the year and how far God has brought them. Therefore, we ask them to write or type their assignments each month on A4 paper, with the monthly session and the relevant questions clearly indicated on them. They need to have their name somewhere visible too, just to help with the binding and sorting at the end of the course... you can imagine, with lots of ladies, it can get very confusing otherwise!

The One-to-One Meetings with Mentors

Obviously it would be pointless to mentor someone if you have no goal or purpose. You need to ask yourself what you want the person you are mentoring to look like as a result of your investment in their life. Look at this quote from Tim Elmore's book, *Mentoring* which I have found very useful in the context of goal-setting.

> Spiritually speaking let me suggest a biblical goal for you and your mentee to pursue. Since Jesus had but one significant prayer request in His three and a half year ministry, it might be good to examine that request and use it as a goal. The passage goes like this:
>
> > The harvest truly is plentiful, but the labourers are few. Therefore, pray to the Lord of the harvest to send out labourers into His harvest.
> >
> > (Matt 9:37–38 NKJV)
>
> Jesus prayed for labourers. In fact, I believe the number one goal of His mentoring of the twelve

was to turn laypeople into labourers. My definition
of a labourer is threefold,

1. An intimate disciple of Jesus

2. Who uses their gifts to advance God's
kingdom, and

3. Who is committed to reproducing other
labourers.

If you work toward this end, you will have made a
significant contribution to God's kingdom in that
person's life. Your goal should include all three
facets of the above definition, and should never fall
short of spiritual reproduction. Your mentee should
eventually be able to mentor someone else.[1]

We have found that these one-to-one monthly meetings are
invaluable in the mentoring process. To meet any less than
once a month is not enough and despite our busy lives, we
must fight for these times together. It is so important to hold
your ladies to account and ensure that dates get put in the
diary at monthly group meetings so that you are set up in
advance for the whole month. To just assume that you will
catch up at some point in the month is short-sighted; before
you know it, the month is past and you have not managed
to meet with each of your ladies. Try to be organized in this
department to avoid future disappointment.

The meetings you have with the person you are
mentoring need to be held in a comfortable and safe setting.
By safe, I mean an atmosphere where honest, transparent
discussion can occur. Initially, you may want to go out
for coffee together, especially if you do not already have
a close relationship but bear in mind that accountability

is best implemented in private. Being in public will limit how freely and openly you can share together. (There is nothing more embarrassing than being in a public place and wanting to sob your heart out.) I recommend that the tissue box is never too far away!

When you sit down to meet, take the initiative to set the tone and the atmosphere of your time together. Ensure that you are well prepared and that you have prayed beforehand that God would lead your time together. Remember to have read through her assignment and pinpointed any specific areas that you think need addressing (see the Resources chapter).

Take time in light conversation to just assess where she is and how things are going in her personal life. Guard against jumping in to "business" mode – remember, they are not another box to tick in your busy day! They are your agenda right now and they need to know it; they need your love even more than your good advice. Although, to begin with, you will be taking the lead in pursuing the relationship, we would expect to see a transition take place over time. As she feels secure, she should begin to initiate and start seeking you out too, preventing things from becoming too one-sided and unbalanced. This is an important part of their spiritual maturity, so encourage them to begin to pursue you when you feel the time is right.

It may be helpful during the first meeting to go over expectations on both sides and to clarify what you both want to get out of your times together. This is important to prevent disappointment or frustration further down the line. It is beneficial here to refer back to the questionnaire that they filled in at their first mentoring meeting which covered their expectations, and will provide you with a useful tool to gauge progress along the way.

Conveying your commitment to them and the potential you see in them helps to lay a good foundation for further meetings. They need to know that you believe in them and are dedicated to walking through the year with them. When we know that others are for us, we can allow ourselves to become vulnerable and face the areas that need changing. For some ladies trust is a major issue, especially if they have been hurt or mistreated in the past. In time they will begin to open up and let you in, as you prove your love and commitment to them. Be patient and persevere!

As the relationship is established, you will have opportunity to speak into her life, to address any difficult issues she may be facing and pray through areas of bondage. This is a joyful and awesome privilege. To be able to stand with a fellow daughter and share in her victories is so rewarding for both of us. To be able to spur on, encourage, cheer and applaud is one of the greatest blessings that we reap in the mentoring process.

However, if you encounter an area that you do not feel qualified or confident to deal with, do *not* rush in and just hope for the best! We are all learning, and if you are not sure how to minister in a particular situation, be honest. Tell your lady that you want some time to seek God before you pray together. Ask other women who are more experienced in that particular area for advice and wise counsel. If you are dealing with major spiritual strongholds, it is very unwise to minister alone and this may be a good time to either invite your co-leader or someone else in leadership with more experience to come on board and join you. Don't let pride or foolishness get you out of your depth in any ministry situation, as this could be harmful to both yourself and the woman involved.

I have been amazed at how open and willing the ladies

have been in the one-to-one times. I think part of this has to do with the fact that they are there by invitation. They have already considered the implications and carefully weighed up the cost. They have usually sought God for His confirmation before committing to the programme and therefore are up for whatever He desires to do in their lives during the year. This puts you, as the mentor, at a huge advantage, because you are not trying to "make something happen". They are already prepared and wanting to embrace what God has for them.

Remember, you are nothing more than a tool in the Father's hand. We do not have all the answers – nor is it wise to pretend that we have. Guard against any form of dependency developing over the year and remember to always be pointing and directing them to Jesus. As their mentor, you want to see them come to a place of wholeness and allowing them to become dependent upon you would be seriously damaging. Successful mentoring sees this process through without you becoming their place of safety. God is their source – not you. Teaching and equipping them to run to Jesus first in any crisis helps protect both parties from an unhealthy dependency.

It is important that throughout the year there is a gradual shift in focus, from self to others, otherwise the year can be very inward-looking and self-centred. The long-term goal of mentoring, for us, is to see the ladies come to a place of wholeness whereby they can then reproduce themselves in the lives of others. It is not an eternal journey of "me"! We all have areas in which we desperately need God to shine His light and bring us out from the darkness. We all need someone we can be honest with, who will stand with us, fight with us, and share in our personal victories and triumphs. This is essential and this is why God puts us in relationship with one another. However, if this was all that the year was about, eventually the whole thing could implode. Our very nature, without His mercy and grace, is to be self-centred individuals. We can learn to feed off this self-gratification and never move on into the promises He has for our lives. We can, if we are not careful, become addicted to ourselves! We need to train our ladies to think beyond themselves and their own little worlds. We need to help them broaden their world view and see past their own needs to the needs of those around them. If we do not do this, I believe we are falling short of what God has called us to do. When God, in His love and tenderness, brings us to a place of freedom, it is not just so that we can enjoy the feeling. He desires us to take that which He has given to us and share it with others. We have been blessed to be a blessing. That is the process. That is the bigger picture. That is what we long to see take root in our ladies' hearts.

The End of Year Mentoring Banquet

This is a wonderful part of the ladies' journeys and symbolizes the end of their year together.   All the mentoring groups come together and share in an evening of celebration, giving testimonies and rejoicing in God's incredible goodness.

Usually this event is organized by the mentoring leaders and is intended to be a special blessing and a way of honouring both our ladies and their Father for what has been accomplished. We usually have a theme, depending on what has emerged throughout the course of the year.

Each lady is given a personal invitation to the mentoring banquet, inviting both herself and a guest, either her husband, or a friend who would like to share in the celebration. It is a formal invite, giving all the necessary details including venue, times, dress code and cost. (The cost needs to cover the price of the venue, the food and any décor needed to make the place look special.)

We usually share a special meal together and see it as a great opportunity to simply bless our ladies and tell them how proud we are of them. You can use outside caterers, hire a venue that provides food, or ask people from your church who are not a part of the evening to cater on your behalf. It depends on your budget and what is most appropriate for your particular group. The first year that we had the banquet, we actually held it on a boat on the River Medway, which was a huge success and very intimate, but only practical with quite small numbers. After the initial year, more space was needed and we have used church halls. We always decorate the hall and spend most of the day setting up the tables and making the place look inviting for our ladies. We are blessed with many creative women in Jubilee and together we put much effort into creating a beautiful atmosphere and environment. The surroundings are an important part of the evening and should not be overlooked. Attention to detail in this particular instance is vital and should be done to excellence to glorify our King. Excellence does not necessarily mean expense. A place can be made to look very striking and attractive on a very small budget! It communicates to the ladies, "You're worth it!" and makes them feel loved and valued. We try to provide a small gift or favour at each of the table settings; small details like menus and name places just add that little extra touch.

If you decide to host the event at your own facility, it may be good to arrange a team or two from your church – people who are not involved in the mentoring – who would be willing to come and serve on the evening. It is great to have some of the men serving the tables! It is also good to organize a set-up and a clearing-up team to help at the beginning and end of the evening.

Every year we have asked each group to prepare a funny skit, song or poem to sum up their journey together, which they then perform on the night. It is a guaranteed laugh and a very entertaining part of the evening.

We try to have some sort of PowerPoint presentation during the course of the evening; this could be linked in with the theme, or just something that ties in with what God has done over the course of the year. A few years ago, we had a "Princess–Warrior" theme and one of the ladies put together a great PowerPoint showing various images that reinforced the theme. It was a real expression of the diversity of woman, both intrinsically feminine and yet strong and tenacious.

On this special evening, we present the ladies with their assignments, which we have bound in booklet form for them to treasure and reflect on in the years to come.

We also ask the ladies to each prepare a personal testimony as part of their last assignment, expressing what God has done in their lives over the year. We can then approach various ladies beforehand and ask them to share their testimonies on the night, if they are willing. This is always very moving and powerful, with plenty of tears and laughter.

> ... they overcame... by the blood of the Lamb and by the word of their testimony...
>
> *(Revelation 12:11, NKJV)*

Often the ladies, although their triumphs are personal, experience huge breakthroughs as they testify publicly and it helps establish new thinking patterns in their lives. There is something powerful about the giving of a testimony and, as we see in this verse, together with the blood of the Lamb, there is a great overcoming that occurs. It is as if something is sealed in the Spirit as we speak out the goodness and faithfulness of God in our lives and give Him the glory that He deserves. We have even had some of the husbands give testimony of the changes they have seen in their wives over the course of the year and, as you can imagine, these have been very powerful and encouraging.

It is always wonderful to hear about how the groups have gelled, how new friendships have developed, how captives have been set free and how walking in accountability has been so life-changing. To hear of lives transformed, strongholds broken, minds renewed and daughters firmly planted in the house of God is more than enough reward and makes every little struggle worthwhile.

Training Up New Leaders

The great thing about our leaders is that they have all been through the mentoring programme, so they have a clear understanding of how it works and what is expected of them. Jesus showed His disciples how to live the life by dwelling in their midst for three years, eating and sleeping with them and showing them visually how to live life differently. It was not merely a teaching-based programme that He came to give them, but rather an impartation of kingdom living which He displayed before their very eyes, up close and personal.

As senior leaders, we like to meet once a month with our leaders on a one-to-one basis to see how they are doing.

We have also found it helpful to give our leaders a questionnaire right at the beginning of the year, so that we can assess their expectations personally, those of their co-leaders, and those of their groups in general. This gives each leader an opportunity to voice any concerns they may have.

As a senior leadership team, we are always looking for, and reading, new resources and material that is relevant to the mentoring year. We also try to provide our leaders with any extra reading material that they may find useful either on a personal level or within the group context.

Each month, the senior leaders visit different groups in the leaders' homes. We like to get there in good time, before the members arrive, so that we can pray with the leaders and support them from the outset of the evening, allowing opportunity to chat through any concerns that they may have. Once the ladies have left the meeting, we stay and give our leaders feedback and advice. This is a really valuable time and enables us to connect with our leaders and see their growth and development throughout the year.

After each monthly meeting, our leaders fill out a feedback form (see the Resources chapter) which they then email to us in order to give us useful insight into how the evening has gone. Again, through this we are able to pick up on any areas of concern quickly and efficiently before things build up or get out of hand.

We have in the past provided our ladies with extra training in the form of personality and character type assessments, which have proved useful in identifying particular areas of strength and weakness. Once these have been identified, we can help the leaders to work on their weaker points and achieve their full potential in their areas of strength.

As part of developing our leaders, we endeavour to give them various challenges and responsibilities that will help them to grow in their capacity as a leader. Rising to these challenges and taking on a new area of delegated responsibility allows them to see and measure their growth in a safe and secure environment. An example of this is with the end of year mentoring banquet. Instead of Heather and me always leading and organizing this event, we like to delegate it to our leaders and give them a chance to take responsibility and experience the pleasure of seeing it succeed. There is such a diversity of creativity amongst our leaders and it is a wonderful opportunity for them to express themselves and take ownership of such a worthwhile event.

NOTE

1 Tim Elmore, *Mentoring*, Indianapolis, Indiana: Wesleyan Publishing House, 1995.

Resources

When we started mentoring, we felt as though we were continually just one step ahead of the ladies. The following resources are by no means a complete list but we trust that they will be of benefit to you, should you wish to embark on this journey.

1. Letter of Invitation
2. Launch Day Programme
3. Personal Questionnaire
4. Meeting Schedule
5. Feedback Form
6. Feedback Questionnaire
7. Meetings and Assignments
8. End of Year Banquet
9. List of Books

1. Letter of Invitation

This letter is used to invite new ladies to be a part of the mentoring programme.

Dear _____

We are writing to invite you to consider being a part of the ladies' mentoring for the coming year.

We have seen God use the mentoring as an incredible tool in building friendships, imparting truth and changing incorrect mindsets. It also provides an opportunity to grow in accountability and internal government.

Your commitment will involve the following:

1. Attending a monthly meeting with your group, held on the first Wednesday of each month.

2. Meeting on a weekly basis with a prayer partner.

3. Reading a prescribed book each month and completing written/practical assignments.

4. Meeting on a monthly basis with your mentor in an accountable relationship.

5. Attending the end of year mentoring banquet.

It is vital that you hear from God before embarking on the mentoring and have a clear sense of His direction. We would be grateful if you could send us a written response explaining why you think you should/shouldn't be a part of the course this year and anything specific you feel He has said to you. You could either give us your response by hand, or email.

We will be launching the mentoring on _____ when we will be spending the day together sharing our hearts regarding the year ahead. The year ends in _____ with a banquet to celebrate God's goodness throughout the year.

We need to have your reply by _____ to help with our planning and preparation.

We look forward to hearing from you.

2. Programme

This is an example of our launch day programme.

09.30   **Welcome**

09.45   **Fun Ice Breaker**

10.00   **Imparting the Heart of Mentoring:**
Heather/Hazel
(What Mentoring is/What Mentoring is not)

10.30   **Discuss various aspects of the commitment:**
• Our expectations
• Monthly meetings
• Prayer partners
• Books
• Assignments

11.00   **Tea/Coffee**

11.30   **Testimonies from previous years**

   Worship
• Press into God – a time of letting go and
surrendering
• Submit the year to the Lord

12.00   **Introduce new mentoring leaders**

12.30   **Lunch**

13.30   **Announce groups – get into groups**
• Share expectations – leaders, then each
member of group
• Complete questionnaires
• Get into prayer partners – introduce one
another
• Arrange first meeting with partners

- Introduce first book
- Hand out first assignment
- Give future dates for monthly meetings plus venue for first meeting

3. Personal Questionnaire

Here is a copy of the detailed mentoring questionnaire that the ladies fill in on the launch day. It is important to make sure these are photocopied prior to the event and that the new leaders have them ready to hand out.

Please answer the following questions as honestly as possible. The information you give will be kept in confidence with your mentoring leader. The purpose of this questionnaire is to access the areas for growth in your life and to help with goal-setting for the year ahead.

Name _____

Address _____

_____

_____

Email _____

Tel. No. (H) _____

(Mobile) _____

Date of Birth _____

Explain briefly why you want to be a part of the mentoring this year:

_____

_____

_____

_____

Kindly tick the box that best describes your situation at present:

	GOOD	OK	NEED GUIDANCE
Your marriage	❏	❏	❏
Your family life	❏	❏	❏
Your spiritual life	❏	❏	❏

Briefly describe how and when you first made a real commitment to the Lord:

_____

_____

_____

_____

How would you describe your walk with Him at the moment?

_____

_____

_____

_____

What do you consider to be the best and the worst aspects of your childhood? What is/was your relationship like with your parents?

_____

_____

_____

Are there any specific issues you are struggling with at the moment?

_____

_____

_____

_____

Please describe which three areas you most struggle to be obedient in.

1. _____

2. _____

3. _____

How well do you think you manage your time? Do you spend your time wisely – are you doing what you want to be doing with your time? Do you think you have a healthy rhythm of work, rest and play?

_____

_____

_____

Are you aware of any unresolved issued regarding your relationships with others that could affect your level of openness and honesty?

_____

_____

_____

How do you respond to God during difficult seasons in your life?

_____

_____

_____

_____

What do you identify as your passion? What are your dreams/aspirations? What do you want to be doing in five years' time?

_____

_____

_____

_____

4. Meeting Schedule

Due to the fact that our leaders are usually mentoring a number of ladies each, we devised the meeting schedule which the leaders use to make brief notes after their one-to-one meetings. We encourage each leader to keep a file containing their ladies' personal details, their questionnaire, their assignments, as well as notes made during their one-to-one times.

| Names: | Date: |
| | Notes: |

| Names: | Date: |
| | Notes: |

5. Feedback Form

The following is a hard copy of the feedback form that the mentoring leaders email through to Hazel and me after the monthly meeting. We have found it extremely beneficial to keep a record of details such as who was there and how the meeting went.

Leaders' names:	Date:
Number of people at meeting:	
Names of ladies who attended:	

Fun Ice Breaker:

Serious Ice Breaker:

Sharing:

Worship:

Impartation:

Announcements:

Reflection of the meeting in general:

6. Feedback Questionnaire

During our final meeting of the year, we ask the ladies to fill in the following questionnaire, as honestly as possible, in order for us to grow in our leadership.

Thank you so much for taking the time to give us this feedback. We appreciate your honesty.

1. What aspects of the year have you particularly enjoyed?

_____

_____

_____

2. How have you grown spiritually? Please give details.

_____

_____

_____

3. Have you grown in your friendships?

_____

_____

_____

4. What do you feel you have gained from your prayer partner relationships?

_____

_____

5. Do you feel as though you were able to effectively pursue your prayer partner(s)?

_____

_____

_____

6. Were you able to share freely, openly and comfortably?

_____

_____

_____

7. Have the assignments contributed towards your growth?

_____

_____

_____

7. Meetings and Assignments

We thought it might be useful to include three examples of our monthly meetings that we ran right at the beginning of the new mentoring year, as well as the assignments that went with each meeting.

MENTORING MEETING: Example 1

Meal:

Leaders to prepare a meal for their groups. Whilst eating, discuss the following:

• Why am I in this room?

• Prayer partners to introduce each other to the group.

Worship:

Worship CD playing in the background

• Ladies to quietly consider their expectations for the year. They need to write down what they long to see God do in their life this year. Place expectations in a sealed envelope and give to the group leaders. These will be handed out again at the final meeting in July.

• Prayer partners to share communion together and pray for one another.

Impartation:

Expectations

- Discuss the importance of having a good and healthy expectation for the year.

- Discuss how previous disappointments can affect our expectation levels.

- Write down your expectations of what you want to see God doing in your life this year.

2 Kings 13:10–19

Hostilities were usually proclaimed by a herald, sometimes by a king or general making a public and formal discharge of an arrow into the enemy's country. Elisha directed Joash to do this, as a symbolical act, designed to intimate more fully and significantly the victories promised to the king of Israel over the Syrians. His laying his hands upon the king's hands was to represent the power imparted to the bow shot as coming from the Lord through the medium of the prophet. His shooting the first arrow eastward – to that part of his kingdom which the Syrians had taken and which was east of Samaria –was a declaration of war against them for the invasion. His shooting the other arrows into the ground was in token of the number of victories he was taken to gain; but his stopping at the third betrayed the weakness of his faith; for, as the discharged arrow signified a victory over the Syrians, it is evident that the more arrows he shot the more victories he would gain.

As he stopped so soon, his conquests would be incomplete.

(Commentary Critical and Explanatory on the Whole Bible)

Write down your expectations of what you want to see God do in your life this year.

- Be specific and set the bar high (if you aim for the stars, you'll at least hit the clouds!).

- Be expectant. Proverbs 21:31 says, "The horse is made ready for the day of battle, but victory rests with the Lord" (NIV). You *will* have your victory.

- Don't let your conquests be incomplete! You want to be able to get at the end of this year and see the extent of your victory. God is *able*, no matter where you're at now!

- Be zealous, eager and hungry to see your enemies destroyed and your issues put to bed.

Remember one thing: God responds to a hungry heart. Are you hungry for this victory? If not, how can you get back at a place of hunger?Start eating again from His Word, of His promises. Refocus and be re-envisioned as to what God can do in your life.

Are you going to negotiate, give in, or set the bar too low?

Are you put off by circumstances around you, or what has been?

Go for it!

Hand out assignment and books

Announcements

MENTORING ASSIGNMENT: Example 1

1. Read *The Return of the Prodigal Son*.

2. Using the Word, find and record Scriptures that reflect the nature and character of God as our Father.

3. Together with your prayer partner, prepare a sketch or drama on the prodigal son ready to present to the group at the next monthly meeting.

MENTORING MEETING: Example 2

Welcome:

Each lady is to bring an item that reflects a facet of their personality. Place the items in a bag and let each lady take one out and guess who the item belongs to. Once you know who the item belongs to, let them explain why they brought it and what it says about them.

Ice Breaker:

Drama on prodigal son. (This was a part of the previous month's assignment.)

Impartation:

Discussion time:

- What do you have to give?

- Lie of the enemy – "I have nothing to give..." Feel like this when we are overwhelmed; tired; lost perspective; over-peopled!

- We do not live life according to our feelings but are led by the Spirit of God (Romans 8:14).

"It is written..."

Acts 20:35: "It is more blessed to **give** than to receive" (NIV, our emphasis).

Matthew 10:8: "Heal the sick, raise the dead, cleanse those who have leprosy, drive out demons. Freely you have **received**, freely **give**" (NIV, our emphasis).

1 Peter 4:10: "Each one should use whatever gift he has received to **serve others**, faithfully administering God's grace in its various forms" (NIV, our emphasis).

Acts 3:6: "Silver or gold I do not have, but **what I have I give you**. In the name of Jesus Christ of Nazareth, walk" (NIV, our emphasis).

- We need to focus on what we do have, rather than not having the silver or gold.

- Not necessarily a physical rising but rising above emotions, circumstances, difficulties.

- Woman who poured perfume onto Jesus' feet. Read handout by Joanna Weaver, Having a Mary Heart in a Martha World.

- Not despising what we have.

- Illustration – Dead Sea – no water leaving – what happens?

- Are we bringing words of life, or words of death?

Practical Application:

Get the ladies to pair up with their prayer partners and to do a word study on the different ways that we can give.

Have concordances, commentaries, study aids and internet – in prayer partners, look at Scriptures and feedback to group their findings on the following areas:

- Words of encouragement/words of life
- Physical giving

- Attitude

- Hospitality (time, attitude, serving)

Ladies to share their findings with the group.

Hand out assignment and books

Announcements

MENTORING ASSIGNMENT: Example 2

1. Write on an A4 sheet, answering the following question: "Who am I?"

It should not refer to your job, ministry, gifting, marital status or family. What defines you?

2. Note the following areas:

- Physical giving

- Hospitality

- Words of life/words of encouragement

- Positive attitude

In which area are you most consistent in making a positive contribution to the lives of others?

Which area do you feel you need to pay attention to?

3. Read and study the book of James.

What particular area do you feel most challenged in? Do an in-depth study on this area. (Use a variety of study aids.) Share with your mentor at your next one-to-one how they can best hold you to account in this area.

MENTORING MEETING: Example 3

Tea/Coffee/Welcome

Ice Breaker:

Each group to prepare something really fun and light-hearted.
Recite Jubilee Church vision statement (learned at previous monthly meeting).

Serious Ice Breaker:

Answer the question: What does it mean to you to walk as a "daughter in the house"?

Impartation:

Discuss the different stages of "sonship".
What does a mature daughter of the King look like?

Guest: Invite a female member of your church leadership team to share testimony on their journey of growing as a daughter in the house. What are the key lessons they have learned along the way?

Groups:

In groups of three or four, share where you feel that you are at in your journey of sonship.

Worship:

Repenting of independence.
Spend time with God, positioning yourself to walk as a daughter of the King.

Announcements:

Prepare and plan next month's travelling supper for your mentoring group.

MENTORING ASSIGNMENT: Example 3

1. Read *The Shack* by William P. Young.

2. Journal as you read. Identify any areas where you have possibly had a warped perception of God as your Father.

3. Go through handout on "Spirit of Sonship versus Spirit of Slavery" (see below). Identify the areas where you recognize in your own life a tendency to operate as a slave rather than as a son.

4. Spend time reading the Word and come prepared to share with the group what you have been reading and what God has been saying to you this month.

No	Spirit of Sonship	Spirit of Slavery
1	Privilege	Cost/Sacrifice
2	Son/daughter	Slave
3	See God as a loving Father	See God as Master
4	Theology: Live by law of love	Theology: Live by love of the law
5	Secure in your identity – can find rest and peace in who you are	Insecure in your identity – no inner peace
6	Need for approval: Totally accepted by God's love and grace	Need for approval: Continually striving for acceptance by people; praise and approval
7	Motivation for serving: Service that is motivated by a deep gratitude for being unconditionally loved and accepted by God. Heart's cry – Abba Father – motivated to please the Father	Motive for serving: A need for personal achievement as you seek to impress God and others (or no motivation to serve at all). Also a sense of fear/duty
8	Source of comfort: Seek times of quietness and solitude to rest in the Father's presence and love	Source of comfort: Seek comfort in counterfeit affections: addictions, compulsions, escapism, busyness, hyper-religious activities
9	Motive for purity: Desire to live a life pleasing to God – do not want anything to hinder an intimate relationship with God	Motive for purity: Must live a life pleasing to God – to earn God's favour. This increases feelings of shame and guilt
10	Self-image: Positive and affirmed because you know you are valued by God	Self-image: Often feelings of rejection as you compare yourself with others

11	Peer relations: Humility and unity as you value others and are able to rejoice in their blessings and success	Peer relations: Jealousy towards others' success and position
12	Handling others' faults: Love covers as you seek to restore others in a spirit of love and gentleness	Handling others' faults: Accusation and exposure in order to make yourself look good by making others look bad
13	View of authority: Respectful, honouring to authority; see authority as ministers of God for good in your life	View of authority: See authority as a source of pain; distrustful towards them and lack a heart attitude of submission
14	View of admonition: See correction as a blessing and need in your life – see it as an opportunity for growth	View of admonition: Difficulty receiving correction – because of your need to be right, your feelings are easily hurt. You tend to close your spirit to discipline
15	Express love openly: It is easy to lay your life and agendas down in order to meet the needs of others	Guarded and conditional in expressing love – based on others' performance as you seek to get your own needs met
16	Sense God's presence as close and intimate	Sense God's presence as conditional and distant
17	Vision: To daily experience the Father's unconditional love and acceptance and then be sent as a representative of His love to family and others	Vision: Spiritual ambition; the earnest desire for some spiritual achievement and distinction and the willingness to strive for it; a desire to be seen and counted among the mature
18	It's the son that gets the inheritance!	Servant merely oversees and runs all that the master demands

| 19 | Irony: There is a cost involved in being a son or a daughter of the kingdom – those who give their lives will gain everything | Those who hold on to their lives will lose them. Matthew 10:39: "Whoever finds his life will lose it, and whoever loses his life for my sake will find it" (NIV). |

8. End of Year Banquet

Here is an example of the end of year banquet programme.

LADIES' MENTORING BANQUET

10.00	Meet at venue to set up tables, decor etc...
19.00	Leaders arrive. Pour drinks; put out chocolates; welcome ladies at door
19.30	Guests arrive. Serve drinks and get ladies and guests seated (background music playing)
19.45	Welcome. Explain why we are here: a celebration of God's goodness
19.50	DVD Proverbs 31 – Princess Warriors (PowerPoint presentation especially prepared for the evening)
19.55	Fun Ice Breaker
20.10	Each group to present their song, poem, drama, or dance (prepared at last mentoring meeting)
20.30	Grace – Dinner (background music playing)
21.00	Testimonies prepared by ladies
21.30	Dessert
22.00	Hand out bound copies of the ladies' assignments. Give small gifts
22.10	DVD – Fun photographs taken throughout the year

9. List of Books

Here is a list of recommended books that we have used over the years.

1. *Celebration of Discipline* – Richard Foster, Hodder & Stoughton, 1998

2. *A Woman After God's Own Heart* – Elizabeth George, Harvest House Publishers, 1997

3. *Captivating* – John and Stasi Eldredge, Thomas Nelson, 2005

4. *Journey into God's Heart* – Jennifer Rees Larcombe, Hodder & Stoughton, 2006

5. *Making Jesus Lord* – Loren Cunningham, YWAM Publishing, 2001

6. *Spiritual Warfare* – Dean Sherman, YWAM Publishing, 2001

7. *Battlefield of the Mind* – Joyce Meyer, Hodder & Stoughton, 2002

8. *Everybody's Normal Till You Get to Know Them* – John Ortberg, Zondervan, 2003

9. *If You Want to Walk on Water, You've Got to Get Out of the Boat* – John Ortberg, Zondervan, 2001

10. *The Life You've Always Wanted* – John Ortberg, Zondervan, 2002

11. *Drawing Near* – John Bevere, Thomas Nelson, 2004

12. *Under Cover* – John Bevere, STL, 2001

13. *Breaking Intimidation* – John Bevere, Charisma House, 2006

14. *A Tale of Three Kings* – Gene Edwards, Tyndale House Publishers, 1992

15. *The Return of the Prodigal Son* – Henri Nouwen, Darton, Longman & Todd, 1994

16. *There is Always Enough* – Heidi Baker, Sovereign Publishing, 2001

17. *Compelled by Love* – Heidi Baker, Charisma House, 1998

18. *God's Favourite House* – Tommy Tenny, Destiny Image Publishers, 2000

19. *God's Secret to Greatness* – Tommy Tenny and Dave Cape, Regal Books, 2000

20. *God on Mute* – Pete Grieg, Kingsway, 2007

21. *Redeeming Love* – Francine Rivers, Monarch, 2004

22. *Lineage of Grace* – Francine Rivers, Tyndale House, 2003

23. *The Heavenly Man* – Paul Hathaway, Monarch, 2003

24. *Becoming a Person of Influence* – John Maxwell, STL, 1997

25. *Safely Home* – Randy Alcorn, Tyndale House, 2003

26. *Making Life Work* – Bill Hybels, Inter-Varsity Press, 2007

27. *The Supernatural Ways of Royalty* – Bill Johnson and Kris Vallotton, Destiny Image Publishers, 2006

28. *The Shack* – William P Young, Hodder Windblown, 2008

29. *What's so Amazing About Grace?* – Philip Yancey, Zondervan, 2002

30. *Having a Mary Heart in a Martha World* – Joanna Weaver, WaterBrook Press, 2000

31. *Be Committed* – Warren W. Wiersbe, David C. Cook, 1992

32. *Humility* – Andrew Murray, Bethany House, 2001

33. *Love as a Way of Life* – Gary Chapman, Hodder & Stoughton, 2008

Daniela's Story

Daniela is a young lady who has been a part of Jubilee Church for the past two years. The growth we have seen in her life has been incredible as she has journeyed the road of discovering her true identity as a daughter of the King. She recently completed an assignment entitled "Who am I?" and it blessed us so much that we asked her if we could include it in this book.

The Princess

Daniela Helfrich

Once upon a time there was a little princess.
In the eyes of the child her father was strong,
Very strong and very rich.
Perfect in his judgment and wisdom.
Like a king, sovereign, ruling her little world.
A king deeply loved and adored by the princess.

As she grew up he taught her a lot of things –
How to work hard as he did, because success would
*   make her rich.*
Even if her heart ached at times, she learnt to hide
*   the pain.*
So did he.
She embraced the rules he gave her to prove her love
*   to him, till it hurt.*
She imitated him as he never allowed himself to fail.

But sometimes it still happened.
She did everything for a simple "I love you."
All he would say was, "You did well."
To be accepted it was important to please – that she
*   learnt quickly.*
And understood that it was not about being a
*   daughter, but about his fulfilled expectations.*

She just wanted to be seen as beautiful – but he
*   disliked it if she drew attention to herself,*
And ignored her effort to be seen as a girl of beauty.
He pointed out her weaknesses – and sometimes her
*   talents.*
Always careful not to encourage too much.
Because he had never known it to be any different.

She loved his strong arms and the comfort they
*   seemed to offer for a hurting little soul.*
But he would ask her to be stronger than she was in
*   the time of broken wings.*
She pleased, she earned, and she strived – just to
*   see herself so often not good enough for him.*
Left behind, rejected or ignored.
He knew too well how that felt.

As the years went by she learnt about guilt and
*   shame.*
She would not run with open arms towards him any
*   more as she once had done.*
He actually missed it – but didn't show it, of course.
She withdrew, didn't dare to look into his eyes
*   to maybe find that they were busy watching*
*   someone else.*

*She started to fear, to mistrust, to lie – and the
joyful flower she had once been created to be,
withered away.*

*He didn't like what he saw, but stood helpless and
hard, just grieving inside.*

*She would even turn her back on him, unwilling to
receive any kind of guidance and correction.*

*One day she left his house, after her heart had
already left him a long time ago.*

His wounded heart was hurt once more.

*She only held on to the little bag she carried, but
even that was too heavy for her.*

*But she had seen him carrying much bigger burdens
all these years, so she didn't even think about it.*

And as she closed the door she finally realized

*She was nothing more than a broken father's broken
daughter.*

*She worked hard. The masters were well pleased
with her.*

She did what she was asked to do. Even more.

*Earned what they had promised her. Sometimes
less, but never more.*

*It was not enough, not worth living for it, but there
was no choice.*

In a desperate moment she finally found Him.

*This king, a very different master, kind and better
than all the others.*

She had passed His door many times.

*But from the very moment she entered His house she
knew, she would never want to leave it again.*

*She actually fell in love with Him. As much as her
  wounded heart would allow it.
One touch from Him would make her broken wings
  desire to fly again.*

*He Himself would take her old heavy bag away and
  show her a room in His house.
One which would belong to her as long as she
  wanted to stay in His house.
The window gave free view over the wide and
  peaceful land He owned.*

*But there was not much time to waste.
No time to sit and enjoy the Master's land.
She did what she was asked to do. As she had
  always done.
She worked. Hard. Long hours. Till exhaustion.
But for some reason she never got tired of it.
It was the love for Him, the Master that kept her
  going.
She couldn't explain, but it empowered her to serve
  Him well. And sometimes even better.*

*She realized He liked her.
He sometimes watched her as she served Him.
His eyes searched for her often, followed her when
  she left the room.*

*But she couldn't allow herself to be carried away.
So much work to do.
There were not enough workers to keep the King's
  expanding household in order.
Not one evening was all the work done.
She was happy to do overtime –*

*Even when sometimes He had asked her to just sit
   and eat with him.*
In fear she would step back.
She was a worker. No more than a slave.
He would observe her restless hands.
*She needed the busyness, the buzz of the vibrant
   working hours.*
*The times when she could do her job and think
   about the Master and how it would be to just sit
   with Him.*
Quietly.
At rest.
In love.

*She was proud to know that she worked harder than
   a lot of the others.*
More effective. Better. Full of passion and love.
*And she hoped He would see how well she served
   Him.*
He would be pleased – she hoped.
But in her heart she was still not sure.

It would have been forever like that.
But one day she found a letter on her bed.
A white, elegant envelope.
It seemed to be an invitation.
*The Master's writing was strong and confident, but
   with a gentle touch it almost seemed.*
So too were His words.

But still – they shattered her world.
And broke her life into pieces once again.

He wrote in simple words:

He would not want and need her services any more.
But that she was welcome to stay in His house.
As long as she wished to.

Her eyes stared at the words in disbelief.
Did He not appreciate what she had done?
All that hard work, the long hours? Her love and
*   devotion?*

Loss and grief seemed to overwhelm her.
Rejection. Not found worthy again.
Shameful tears cried in the dark nights.
She stayed in her room, unable to face anybody.
Not Him. Not others.
She hid for days. Weeks.
Till she even felt there was nothing to hide any
*   more.*
Who would try to hide a nobody?

He did not come.
Of course not.
He had nothing to explain. To make her understand.
To thank her. Or even to send her away.
Nothing.
It was his right to make a decision like that.

It felt like a small eternity.
Life was suddenly limited and captured inside four
*   white walls and a low ceiling.*
Nowhere to go. Nowhere to turn.
Nothing to do.
Her always busy, restless hands became still.
Resting on her lap, doing nothing.

*After many days, it felt like forever, she picked up
      that letter again.*
For the first time after that dark day
She read again His words to her.
*The first and the last ones he had ever written to
      her.*

*In the desperation and distress of that past day,
      she had not even been able to finish reading his
      words.*
Now she finally did.

*And as they did on that day, so too this time did his
      words change her life again and forever. As she
      went down to what was written at the end of the
      page.*
She had not even noticed what it said:

"You are My princess.
*A King's daughter's destiny is not to work for the
      King, but her place is at the King's side.*
*I want you to be what you are, My daughter,
      somebody who inherits all that is Mine.*
Come downstairs as soon as you are ready.
I will be waiting for you.
I love you My beautiful one.
Dad"

*It was only a short time later, as a princess, silently
      and shy she climbed down the stairs of the
      King's majestic palace.*
Her eyes were full of tears.
Her heart still fearful to believe.

*All she carried in her once so busy hands was a
 letter.*

*Handwritten by her former Master, now her King,
 her Father.*

*It was her only proof, the only truth she could stand
 on.*

Would He remember His words? His promise to her?

*The floating silk of the long, simple, but royal dress
 she wore, felt good.*

*She had found it in the cupboard she had never
 dared to open.*

*Was this really what she should have been since the
 very beginning?*

*Even in that moment it would have been so much
 more natural for her to kneel down.*

Brush the wooden floor. Sweep the stairs.

But she didn't pause. Think. Or stand still.

She walked towards the throne room.

*Her hand shook as she closed it around the golden
 handle of the heavy doors.*

*With the other she pressed the letter, His word to
 her, closer to her body.*

Would He still feel the same about her?

*As she opened the door, all doubt, all questions were
 driven out of her heart.*

*It was as if the warmth of His tender love floated
 from the throne towards her.*

Reached her. Surrounded her.

The stream reflected the dawn of a new day.

*No word was spoken between them, but His eyes
 met hers.*

And as He smiled she felt like He would hold her
heart in His hands.
She took a deep breath. The air filled her lungs.
Like the assurance filled her very being:
Here was her place.
She was the King's daughter.
Nothing to fear any more as He welcomed the
princess she was and had always been.
Totally accepted and embraced by an eternal Father.

Only as she took her rightful place at the King's
side, did she realise:
She had lost a duty.
And gained a kingdom.

She had lost her strife to be found worthy of love.
And captured the king's heart.

She had lost her position
And found her identity.

She had lost her earning
And found her security.

She had lost her busyness.
And found rest forever.

Never again would she need to do what a broken
world had taught her.
But she would be beautiful for the kingdom.
She would dance with the King.
Dance in His unforced rhythms of grace.